Chinese Regular Script Calligraphy for Beginners

Zong Jianye

Translated by Wen Jingen with Pauline Cherrett

FOREIGN LANGUAGES PRESS

Third Edition 2012

Text by Zong Jianye
English translation by Wen Jingen with Pauline Cherrett
Designed by Cai Rong
Art by Zong Jianye, Sun Shuming Wen Jingen

Chinese Regular Script Calligraphy for Beginners

ISBN 978-7-119-04861-1
© 2007 by Foreign Languages Press
Published by Foreign Languages Press
24 Baiwanzhuang Road, Beijing, 100037, China
Home page: http:// www.flp.com.cn
Email address: info@flp.com.cn
sales@flp.com.cn
Distributed by China International Book Trading Corporation
35Chegongzhuang Xilu, Beijing 100044, China
P. O. Box 399, Beijing, China

Printed in the People's Republic of China

Contents

Translator's notes:

1. All illustrations in this book were executed and provided by the author unless otherwise stated. 书中未注明作者的图片均为本书作者所作。

2. To make this book more accessible for non-Chinese readers, the translator has extensively edited the original text, and added some illustrations. The translator, and not the author, is responsible for all errors accruing from any rewriting and rearrangement.

为适应外国读者需要，本书编译过程中对原作的图文做了一定改动。着粪续貂，在所难免；所生舛误，咎在译者。敬希作者及读者见谅。

Omnipresent Chinese calligraphy

Today Chinese calligraphy is seen everywhere. It carries within it a history. It currently exists and it also extends to the future.

Gate of the ancestral temple of Family Pei, in a village of northern China

How could Zhao Mengfu who died in 1322 inscribe a board over the gate to a Beijing's park today? People collected these characters for the name of the park from Zhao's calligraphic works to make this tasteful panel.

These inscriptions on rock in a tourist attraction in the southernmost island of China were done by men of letters in the past.

Panel of an ancient temple in the western outskirts of Beijing shows graceful calligraphic achievements.

The panel of an artists' shop in today's Liulichang Street, Beijing, was written by Weng Tonghe (1830 — 1904), the instructor of the Qing-dynasty emperor Guangxu (r. 1875 — 1909).

Gateway in a village of
northern China

Hanging couplet (written by Beijing calligrapher Liu Ruizhen)
on either side of a gate

Wangfujing Street lined with old and new shops, downtown Beijing

The shop sign of the famous roast duck restaurant Quan Ju De, Beijing

A small shop which produces inscribed panels and shop signs
for customers, Liulichang Street, Beijing

德勝 國際

CHINA
TRIUMPHAL ARCH

6237 6688/9988

建设集团 发展商:北京德胜投资有限责任公司

Construction site of a new high-rise block.
Photographs pp.5-16 by Wen Jingen

Introduction

Wen Jingen

I suppose you are interested in Chinese language and culture. You may have learnt some Chinese characters. Right? You will certainly have found that Chinese characters are more "difficult" than the letters in your own language, but also that well-written Chinese characters are very beautiful. It is high time that you start to learn regular script calligraphy.

In ancient civilisations, the writing signs for many people were pictographs. These were "pictures" that stood for some words or phrases. Chinese people began to use such signs about six thousand years ago. Some writing systems in the world later evolved into phonetic symbols, but the Chinese have used pictographs until today. Of course during the past millennia Chinese characters have undergone many changes.

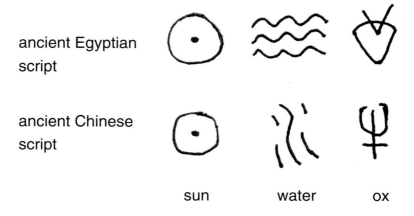

ancient Egyptian script

ancient Chinese script

sun   water   ox

Ancient Egyptian and Chinese characters for sun, water and ox. Illustration by Wen Jingen

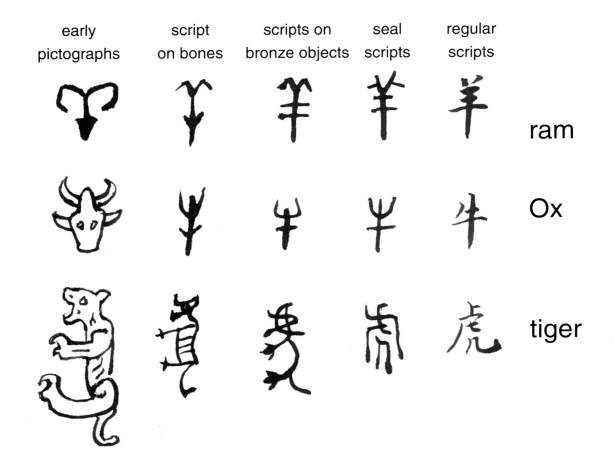

early pictographs	script on bones	scripts on bronze objects	seal scripts	regular scripts	
					ram
					Ox
					tiger

Evolution of Chinese writing: several stages from pictures to characters. Illustration by Wen Jingen

Different styles of Chinese calligraphy (seal script and official script belong to early stages of Chinese writing; the running and cursive scripts are shorthand styles.) Illustration by Wen Jingen

Seal	Official	Regular	Running	Cursive	
水	水	水	水	水	water
兵	兵	兵	兵	兵	soldier
木	木	木	木	木	tree
犬	犬	犬	犬	犬	dog
泉	泉	泉	泉	泉	fountain
居	居	居	居	居	dwell
友	友	友	友	友	friend
夜	夜	夜	夜	夜	night

No one knows the exact date when the regular script came into being. Scholars agree that between the 1st and 2nd century it began to be widely used. Over last two thousand years this script has been the major form of writing in China and it has been in a comparatively constant form.

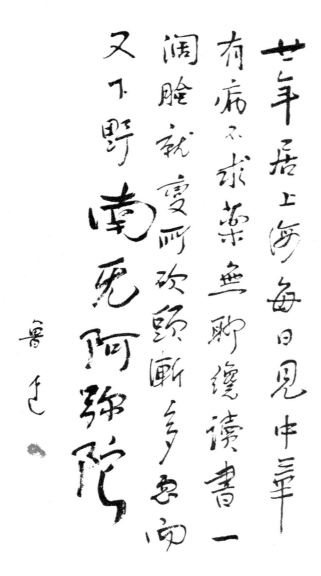

A poem by Lu Xun (1881-1936) written in his own hand. Lu Xun, a literary giant in 20th-century China, is also a good calligrapher.

Calligraphy is a universal art but in China it may attract more attention than in other countries. During the imperial period in China, all scholars used the brush to write documents. Over time they learned to manipulate the soft-tipped brush and thereby developed their unique aesthetic principles concerning handwriting. On one hand calligraphy served a practical purpose and on the other, it became an independent branch of art. Today Chinese calligraphy still serves these two purposes.

The use of the brush for calligraphy compliments the softness of the Chinese landscape, and the agricultural pursuits of the people, as opposed to the use of the stylus or pen in the dry, barren landscape of Mediterranean countries with the use of stone for buildings and monuments.

Everywhere in China you see calligraphy: in people's homes, on shop signs, in public places, at various ceremonies, as presents given to friends and relatives or to foreign visitors. So long as people need to write with a pen or brush, it is necessary to learn calligraphy, because writing Chinese characters is not as easy as writing letters in an alphabet. With some training and practice, you will write a neat and easily recognisable hand. This will greatly facilitate your communication in the Chinese language. Besides, practising calligraphy helps you to develop a careful work style. If you make further progress and develop an interest in the art of calligraphy, you will benefit greatly. Through calligraphy you will have a better understanding of Chinese art and culture.

To teach school children good handwriting does not mean that we want them all to become calligraphers. We want to let them write characters in accordance with the norms, to write correctly, neatly and recognisably. To cultivate such a habit has an advantage — to encourage people to be careful, to let them concentrate their will on the job in hand, to get them to be considerate for other people. Hasty, careless and arbitrary work style tends to bungle matters. To practise calligraphy helps to avoid such bad habits.

— Guo Moruo (1892-1977), poet, dramatist, calligrapher, historian and late president of China Academy of Sciences

Why the Regular Script?

Most Chinese calligraphers agree that students of calligraphy should begin with the regular script. The reason is clear — regular script is used today, whilst seal script and official script are obsolete — they are not used in daily communication. Running script and cursive script are used but they are just shorthand forms of the regular script. If we compare the regular script to walking, then running script and cursive script are running. One cannot run before one learns to walk.

Factors for Good Calligraphy

There are too many theoretical works on Chinese calligraphy for a beginner to read and digest. In practice one can approach calligraphy from its basic elements: the stroke and the structure.

Component: stroke

To produce a good stroke, one must control the brush and move it steadily. (Of course, it takes time to learn to control the brush.) Though the brush may sometimes move a little faster or slower, the change of speed should also be steady. A stroke produced by a well-controlled brush looks full, robust and yet supple. On the other hand, a poorly controlled brush produces weak and insipid strokes. Just like driving a car, if you keep your car under your control, it should move steadily from the beginning to the end. You go straight and make turns; you speed it up and slow it down but without a jerk or bump.

Chinese calligraphers consider strokes in the following shapes undesirable. They are like jerks or bumps of a car in motion:

Illustration by Wen Jingen

In this illustration, the faulty strokes on the top line, from left to right, are respectively named as "nail's cap", "mouse's tail", "wasp's waist" and "crane's knee". The normal shapes of those strokes should be:

Illustration by Wen Jingen

All these faulty strokes stem from a brush out of control. Strength is applied unevenly: a sudden start and an abrupt bounce, and a feeble finish or a thumping drop.

With these sick strokes in mind, you will better understand the ways of brush movement as explained in this book.

Chinese Characters and Their Radicals

Some Chinese characters are "blocks" — you cannot break them up. Examples are: 人 (human), 工 (work), 土 (earth), 大 (large), 口 (mouth), 日 (sun), 木 (wood), 月 (moon), 目 (eye), 刀 (knife), etc. Many characters, however, consist of two or more parts. These constituents are called "radicals". Usually, a radical may serve as indication of the meaning or the pronunciation of the whole character. For example, the character 明 meaning "bright" has two radicals, 日 (sun) and 月 (moon). Since both the sun and the moon are bright, the character consisting of the two radicals has the meaning "bright". Another example, 吐 (vomit, pronunciation: tu) has one radical 口 (mouth) showing that the character is related with the mouth (sure, you vomit through your mouth!) and the other radical 土 whose pronunciation is "tu" too. Study of the radicals helps to make the origin of characters clear.

For a student of calligraphy, to write radicals well is a step to writing characters well.

Structure

The key to a good structure is balance. Just as Chiang Yee says, "although our ancient masters doubtless had no knowledge of mechanics, most of their characters succeed in obeying its laws! The centre of gravity, for instance, is always rightly placed." (*Chinese Calligraphy*, Harvard University Press, 1972, p. 117)

The centre of gravity must fall on a base. Otherwise, the character will totter and collapse.

日下人飞乙成女上
日下人飞乙成女上

Illustration by Wen Jingen

The characters on the top line have their centre of gravity correctly placed. The centre of gravity of characters on the bottom spread beyond the base so these characters appear tottering.

The space between strokes in a character should be largely the same. If some strokes have a wide space between them while others have a narrow space between them, the character looks out of balance.

Illustration by Wen Jingen

The characters on the bottom line have uneven spaces among strokes, so they look out of balance.

But exact symmetry is not preferable. One tries to achieve slight variations between the left and the right, the top and bottom of a character. For example, the right end of a horizontal stroke is a bit higher than the left end. The three horizontal strokes of the character 三 are not of the equal length, the top stroke is long, the middle stroke shorter, and the bottom stroke the longest. The two radicals 木 in the character 林 are not of the same height, the right one higher than the left one. The character 竹 has two radicals 个. If you repeat the same radical 个 twice, the left and the right halves collide each other. Reduce the last stroke of the left radical a little to make way for the right radical and the whole character looks comfortable.

Illustration by Wen Jingen

To keep radicals of a character in balance, one should treat the same radical in various characters in different ways. You may visualise a character or radicals in a character posing certain stances or gestures. For example, the radical 子 is written differently in 孙, 好 and 学. In the character 孙 and 好, the last stroke of the left radical 子 and 女 extends towards the first stroke of the right radical 小 and 子, as if two people are extending their hands to each other, giving a balanced stance. On the other hand, in the character 学 the lower radical 子 should keep its left and right ends poised, otherwise the centre of gravity tilts to the left and the whole character appears unstable.

Illustration by Wen Jingen

The radicals in the characters on the second line look awkward, because they are not in "corresponding gestures".

Illustration by Wen Jingen

The character 1 is well composed, with an extended long stroke (at the arrow). When it appears as a radical in another character (2) it should give way to the other radical by shortening its long stroke at the arrow. Otherwise, the two radicals will either push each other, leaving an unsightly large space (A) as in 3, or collide with each other as in 4.

Instead of absolutely equal spaces among strokes, the top of a character may be slightly "tighter" than the bottom.

Illustration by Wen Jingen

The characters on the top line are well-composed. The characters on the middle line have a tight top. Though not in perfect structure, they look better than the characters with a tight bottom on the bottom line.

To keep the character in better balance, some strokes may "stand out" of the whole character:

Illustration by Wen Jingen

Aesthetics

While building a beautiful structure by putting together various strokes, spontaneity is stressed. Just as Chiang Yee points out, "Neatness, regularity and exactitude of outline, such as are found in English or Chinese printing types, are not desirable qualities in Chinese calligraphy." (*Chinese Calligraphy*, p. 117)

Ancient Chinese artists did not explain their aesthetic principles with precise definitions as ancient Greek scholars did. Instead, they used figurative metaphors to expound their aesthetic ideas. These figurative expressions may sound strange to you at first, but once you are familiar with them, you will feel they are pertinent comparisons. For example, Chinese calligraphers compare a good stroke to "chiselling marks in sand". Just imagine you hold a chisel vertically and draw a line in sand, the point of the chisel cuts deep into the sand while its sides push the sand aside to make a mark that contains a clear-cut centre. If you produce a good centre-tip stroke, the point of the brush tip "cuts" at the centre of the stroke just as the point of a chisel does in sand. You feel the centre of the stroke is hard and muscular while the surface is a bit gentler yet at the same time very tough. A good stroke is also compared to a "seal impression in paste". Imagine you press a seal onto the paste and what an impression it will leave! The centre of every stroke is distinct while its outline is irregular. But the irregularity is not deliberately designed. It comes into being "by itself". As for a bending stroke, it should be executed as if you "bend a hairpin". If you bend a hairpin made of a metal, you must exert strength all along it. You can feel that the bent hairpin exudes sturdiness everywhere in it. None of these comparisons give you a definite shape of a stroke. Chinese calligraphers never strive to make their strokes resemble anything in nature — they just evoke in your imagination the "feel" of good strokes. Here the measurement does not matter, but the "spirit" of your stroke does.

There are other comparisons concerning strokes, the structure of characters and those concerning the composition of a piece of calligraphic work. They are the quintessence of ancient Chinese calligraphers' wisdom. I do not advise beginners to delve into such metaphors. Rather, I recommend that they be enlightened by ancient Chinese calligraphers' way of drawing inspiration from life and nature. An ancient calligrapher made a breakthrough in calligraphy after watching a celebrated dancer dancing with a sword. Withered canes hanging on crags inspired another calligrapher. If you study calligraphy and at the same time turn your eye to things beyond, you will one day attain a similar level of enlightenment.

Cultivate your response

Just as James Cahill states quoting Abraham Kaplan, "Art is mostly a cultivated response". (Jason Kuo, *Discovering Chinese Painting*, Kendall/Hunt Publishing Company, 2000, p. 68) Needless to say, it takes time to cultivate your response to the beauty contained in Chinese calligraphy. There is no ready answer to the question of how to develop your understanding of Chinese calligraphy. It seems nothing in Chinese calligraphy can be defined in clear-cut terms. But on the other hand, nothing in Chinese calligraphy is mysterious or incomprehensible either. If you persist in practising handwriting, view and study calligraphic masterpieces from time to time, and try to conceive the "life" and "spirit" contained in them, you will eventually become a virtuoso. In the study of calligraphy, the old adage that "beauty is in the eye of the beholder" holds. You may find a piece of calligraphy beautiful at the first sight. But as you view it again and again over a long time, you will discover more and more beauty in it, just as a lover of

Beethoven will constantly find more beauty within his music. Facing a calligraphic masterpiece, with your own experience accumulated in writing, you will by and by learn to conceive how the creator of a masterpiece wielded his brush, how he or she exerted his or her energy and how he or she infused their feelings into each stroke. This procedure is in effect intercommunication between you and the ancient masters.

Again, remember Chiang Yee's words, "Chinese calligraphy — a lively conception of some equilibrium of forces — can only be achieved by concentrated and unremitting scholarly study." (*Chinese Calligraphy*, p. 132)

I clearly understand that not every reader of this book intends to become a calligrapher and that different readers will achieve varying results. However, even if you do not attain the desired achievement in the study of Chinese calligraphy, your learning process will be a rewarding scholarly experience for you. Your calligraphy may be inferior to that you imitate, but your handwriting will certainly be above the average level. While your hand may not perform perfectly, your understanding of the art of calligraphy will be greatly improved. Even if you cannot become a great producer, you can become an appreciator. If Albert Einstein can claim that music inspires him in his study of the theory of relativity (though so far nobody can verify music as a basis for physics), what you achieve from learning Chinese calligraphy is far more closely and directly related with academic and artistic branches such as Chinese painting, Chinese literature and Chinese folklore. Your cultural vision will be tremendously expanded. And who knows if you will be inspired by Chinese calligraphy in your study of other things? So whether you learn Chinese calligraphy as a hobby or delve into it deeply, your efforts will be repaid handsomely.

A Few Leading Regular Script Calligraphers

China has too many calligraphers for a beginner to know all their names. Years ago, when the brush was the main writing instrument, nearly all scholars knew calligraphy. Many poets, writers, officials, artists, doctors and generals were at the same time calligraphers. Here only a few leading figures are listed.

It is believed that the regular script came into being no later than the 2nd century. The earliest extant regular script work, however, was done by Zhong You (AD 151 — 230).

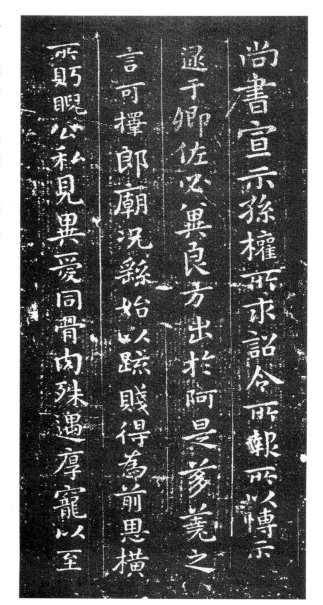

Calligraphy by Zhong You

Wang Xizhi (AD 303 — 361 or 321 — 379) brought this style of calligraphy to an independent and perfect form. He has been praised as a "sage calligrapher".

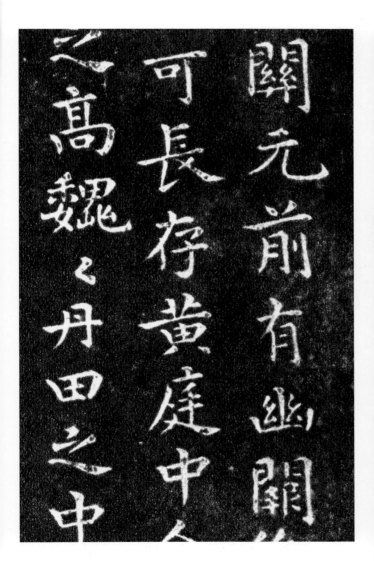

Calligraphy by Wang Xizhi

During the period of the Northern and Southern dynasties (AD 386 — 589), many inscribed stones were erected in China, while other inscriptions were carved on rocks in mountains. Because the inscription style of the Northern Wei (AD 386-534) was excellent, this style of calligraphy is called Wei-stele Style (*wei bei ti* 魏碑体[體]), as exemplified by Zhang Menglong's Stele.

Inscription on Zhang Menglong's Stele

Round stroke and square stroke 方笔[筆]，圆笔[圓筆]

If you start a stroke by pressing the brush tip on the paper and moving it along, the head of the stroke looks square. If you start a stroke by turning the brush tip against the direction of the stroke, the end of the stroke looks round.

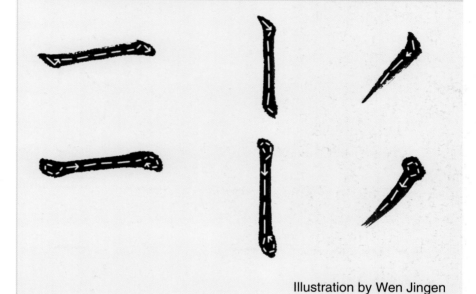

Illustration by Wen Jingen

The strokes on the top are "square strokes". The ones on the bottom are "round strokes". The dotted line shows the track of the brush point.

From the 7th century to the 10th century, regular script calligraphy became more mature with many outstanding calligraphers emerging. Of those calligraphers, Ouyang Xun (AD 557 — 641), Yan Zhenqing (AD 709 — 785) and Liu Gongquan (AD 778 — 865) exerted the greatest influence on later calligraphers.

Ouyang Xun's calligraphy is noted for neat, square strokes and rigorous structure.

Calligraphy by Ouyang Xun

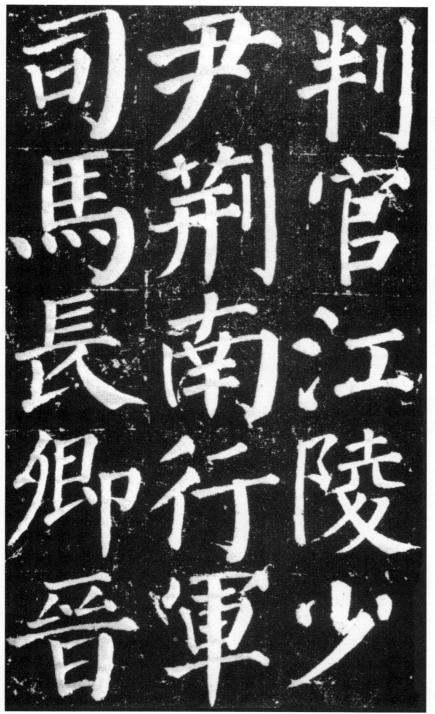

Yan Zhenqing's calligraphy is robust and imposing. His strokes are much rounder than Ouyang Xun's. His calligraphy has been praised for its "tendon".

Calligraphy by Yan Zhenqing

Liu Gongquan drew on Ouyang Xun's strokes and Yan Zhenqing's structure and thus created his own style noted for vigour and openness. Usually the centre of his character is dense and the outer part extending. His calligraphy has been praised for its "bones".

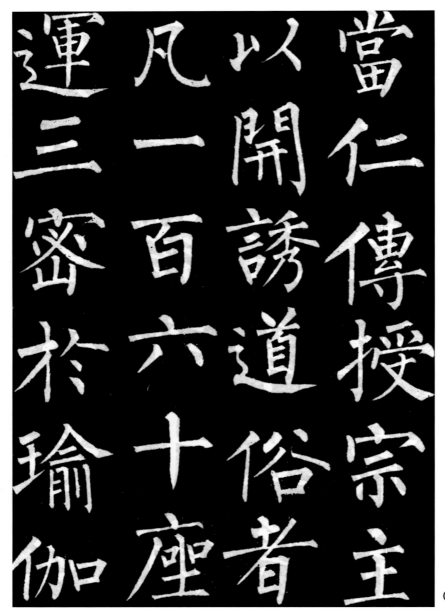

Calligraphy by Liu Gongquan

Since the 11th century, the regular script calligraphy seems to have made little progress. However, there are still some accomplished calligraphers. Zhao Ji (1082 — 1135), or Emperor Huizong of the Song Dynasty (an incompetent ruler who lost his territory to invaders but who was a talented artist) created his own "Slim Golden Calligraphy" (*shou jin ti* 瘦金体[體]).

Calligraphy by Zhao Ji

The multi-talented artist Zhao Mengfu (1254 — 1322) used more square strokes than round. His calligraphy is graceful and spontaneous. Zhao was a member of the imperial family of the Song Dynasty, but as the dynasty fell, he served in the court of the Mongolian conquerors. For this he has been criticised for lack of national integrity and maybe because of this his calligraphy has been criticised as lacking vigour. Whether it is fair to judge his calligraphy by his personality has been a topic of debate.

Despite the huge number of calligraphers and calligraphic styles, works of the "four masters", namely, Ouyang Xun, Yan Zhenqing, Liu Gongquan and Zhao Mengfu, have been taken as models for beginners. Though you may learn calligraphy from other masters too, you should know that not all good calligraphic works can serve as models. Copying generally accepted masterworks is a safe starting point.

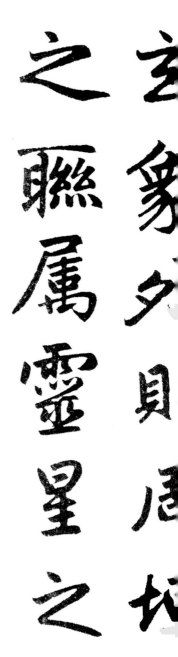

天地闔闢運乎
鴻樞而乱坤爲
之戶日月出入
経乎黄道而卯
酉爲之門是故
遑後林宮羣惡

Calligraphy by Zhao Mengfu

Tools

Brush. The writing brush has been used by Chinese people for thousands of years. There are hundreds of varieties of brushes.

In terms of the fibre in the tip, Chinese writing brushes fall into three categories: stiff-fibre brush, soft-fibre brush and mixed-fibre brush. The stiff fibre brush has a tip made of the hair of weasel, hare, deer or hog. The soft fibre brush uses hair of goat or occasionally, of chicken feather. The tip of a mixed fibre brush is made of both stiff and soft hair such as

Brushes and a brush roll (a mat made of split bamboo to wrap the brushes to protect them during travel). Photograph by Wen Jingen

weasel and goat. The names of the last type include *zi yang hao* 紫羊毫 (purple hare and goat), *wu zi wu yang* 五紫五羊 (half purple hare and half goat), *wu lang wu yang* 五狼五羊 (half weasel and half goat), *qi zi san yang* 七紫三羊 (seven tenths purple hare and three tenths goat), etc.

In terms of the length of the brush tip, brushes are divided into long-tipped, medium-tipped and short-tipped brushes.

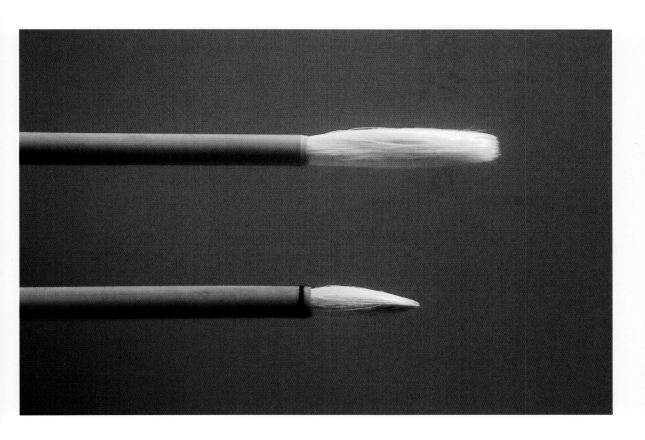

Long tip and short tip brushes. Photograph by Wen Jingen

A good brush has four "virtues". Its tip is sharp, full, flush and resilient — namely when it is loaded, it has a sharp point. When the loaded brush tip is pressed flat, all the fibres finish flush at the end. Its tip is full, forming a perfect cone. If you press the brush tip on paper and then raise it, it resumes to its former shape.

Chinese Regular Script Calligraphy for Beginners

Bad

Good

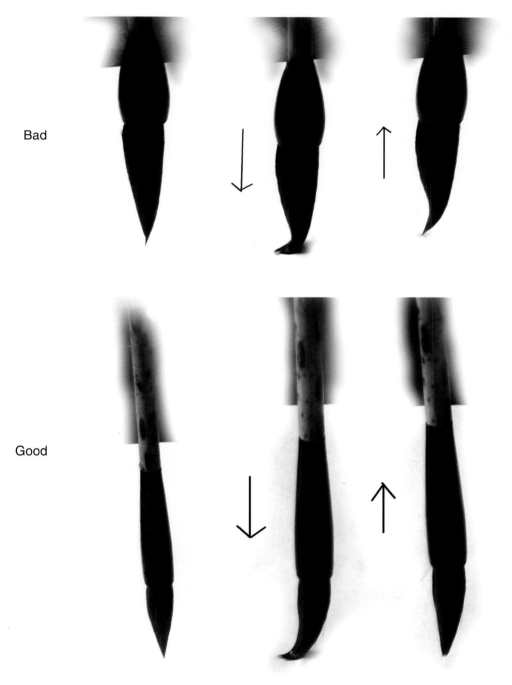

Good and bad brushes.
Illustrations by Wen Jingen

Using a new brush

If the fibres in the tip of a new brush are not glued together, just start using it. First wet the brush thoroughly in clean water, squeeze out the water, and then load it with ink and apply it to the paper.

However, if a new brush has a glued tip (the fibres are sealed with alum or resin for the purpose of safe transportation), you can dip the brush in half a cup of lukewarm water. Leave it in the water for a while and the alum or resin in the tip will be removed. You can now use it.

Load your brush with proper ink. If the ink is too thick, you cannot move your brush smoothly and the resulting characters look dull and cumbersome. If the ink is too thin, the characters produced look fragile and insipid. Also, if you move your brush quickly, you may load your brush with more ink than when you move it slowly.

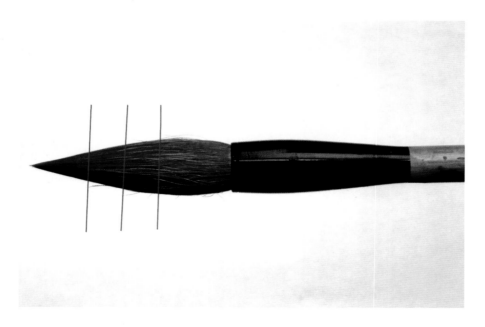

Illustration by Wen Jingen

From the point to the belly a brush tip can be divided into three parts. When you produce a thick stroke, you can press the tip until the third line on the belly. When you produce a thin stroke, you use just the first and the second parts of the tip. Never press the brush tip down to its heel. **It is better writing small characters with a large brush than writing large characters with a small brush.**

Always stroke the brush across a palette, tile or the lid of the ink stone to make sure all fibres lie adjacent to each other and a good point is formed.

Stroking the brush across the lid of the ink stone. Photographs by Wen Jingen

After using, you must wash your brush. Then you can leave it horizontally to dry, or better still, hang it with its tip downwards on a brush hanger and leave to dry. You must straighten and smooth the hairs in the brush, otherwise the fibres will dry in a tangle and the brush will not perform well.

Brushes on a brush hanger. Photograph by Sun Shuming

Ink. For thousands of years Chinese scholars used ink produced by grinding an ink stick with water on an ink stone. In the past this kind of ink stick was erroneously called "Indian ink" in the West.

There are two major types of ink sticks. Those made from soot collected by burning pine wood are called "pine soot ink" (*songyan* 松烟[煙]) and those made from soot collected by burning oil (mainly tung oil), "oil soot ink" (*youyan* 油烟[煙]). The latter is more lustrous than the former. But cheap ink sticks available in the market nowadays are neither "pine soot" nor "oil soot" ink sticks — they are by-products of the petrochemical industry.

Grind your ink with clean water. Do not use tea, warm water or unclean water. When you grind an ink stick, exert some pressure but move the ink stick slowly. Do not put too much water in the ink stone, otherwise the stick will become soaked and may break up.

To save time, nowadays many people use bottled liquid ink. Good brands of liquid ink include *Yi de ge* 一得阁[閣](ink produced in Ye De Ge factory of Beijing), *Zhonghua* 中华[華] (China ink), *Cao Sugong, Hu Kaiwen* 曹素功，胡开[開]文 (inks named after famous ink producers Cao Sugong and Hu Kaiwen) and others.

Ink. Photograph by Sun Shuming

Paper. Paper emerged about two thousand years ago. Nowadays most Chinese calligraphers use a "Xuan paper". It is so named because it was believed to be originally produced in Xuancheng, Anhui Province. But some Xuan papers may be made only in the vicinity of Xuancheng or merely using the same materials and procedure. There are no less than 60 varieties of "Xuan paper" and these may be sized or unsized. The sized Xuan paper is used for producing meticulous style painting and writing.

Beginners can use cheap paper like *maobian zhi* 毛边[邊]纸 (paper made from bamboo pulp) and *yuanshu zhi* 元书[書]纸 (Yuanshu paper) paper instead of Xuan paper. You may use other paper so long as it can absorb ink and is not water resistant. Papers with a slippery and water-resistant surface like those used for photocopy machines and computer printers are not suitable.

In recent years a new kind of rewritable paper ("Magic Paper", *shuixie zhi* 水写[寫]纸 "water writing paper") has been available in the market. You can load your brush with clear water instead of ink and write on such paper. When the characters are wet, they look exactly like on Xuan paper. But after a couple of minutes, the characters dry and become invisible; the paper then resumes its former colour and shape. Thus you can use the paper repeatedly so it is an economical choice. Usually sheets of such paper are bound into a pad and guidelines are often given on the opposite page. Some pads have model characters printed in outlines for the student to copy.

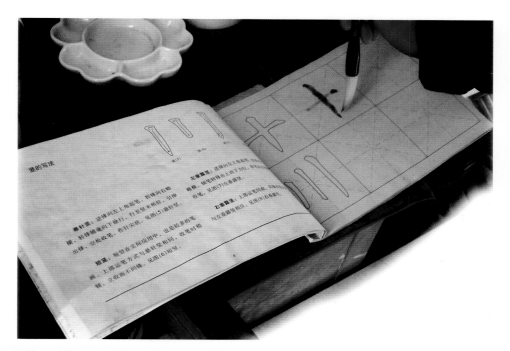

Write with a brush loaded in clean water and you will see the clear character on the rewritable paper.

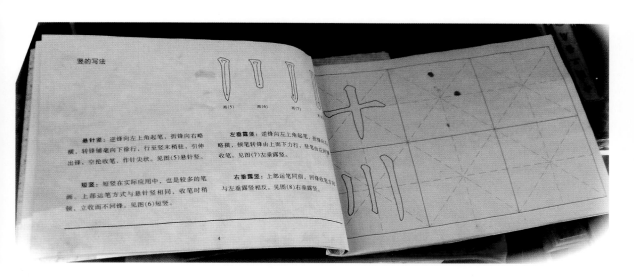

After a while, the water marks are dry and invisible. Photographs by Wen Jingen

Ink stone. The ink stone is used for grinding the ink stick. It is also for holding the ground ink and for stroking the brush fibres so as to make them straight and adjacent to each other. An ink stone may be made of one piece of stone (or other material), or with a lid (of the same material as the base or of wood). Nowadays as bottled ink instead of an ink stick is widely used, the ink stone is less important as it used to be. After use you must wash your ink stone clean.

A good ink stone feels soft and smooth but not slippery. Famous ink stones include those from Duanxi, Guangdong Province, hence the name *duan yan* 端砚(硯), those from Wuyuan, Jiangxi Province (formerly part of Shexian, Anhui Province, hence the name *she yan* 歙砚[硯]), those from Taohe River, Gansu Province, hence the name *tao yan* 洮砚(硯), and others. A baked sedimentary-clay version of an ink stone has been used too.

Some ink stones are exquisitely designed, carved and ornamented, or are made of expensive materials like jade. They are more handicraft articles than artists' instruments.

When you set out your table, put the ink stone on the right, at the far end but within easy reach of your hand when you load or stroke out your brush.

Ink stone. Photograph by Wen Jingen

A piece of **felt** is also necessary if you write on unsized paper. Put the felt under your paper when you write, otherwise the ink will run through your paper, wet the table, come back into your paper and smudge.

Felt. Photograph by Wen Jingen

Get Ready for Writing

Postures:

Correct posture not only ensures good handwriting, but also positively influences your health. That is why a calligrapher must keep a correct posture. Writers mainly keep in one of two positions — sitting or standing. When writing medium-sized and small characters, the writer may use a sitting posture. This posture is usually assumed by beginners.

When you sit to write, you should keep your head facing forward, your back straight, your arms in front of you and your feet comfortably flat on the ground.

When you write large characters, you will do better standing upright. When in this position, keep your feet shoulder distance apart and your right foot maybe half a step in front. The upper half of your body may lean slightly forward. Wield the brush with your right hand and hold the paper with your left. Your right elbow is kept above the table. This posture helps you to complete a coherent piece of calligraphy.

In either posture, you must not feel strained in any part of your body.

Sitting and standing postures.
Photographs by Wen Jingen

Holding the brush correctly

Photographs by Wen Jingen

Hold the brush vertically. There is no sacrosanct rule concerning the way of holding the brush. The guiding principle is that the brush should be held so that the writer can wield it with ease. Chinese calligraphers hold the brush vertically, though the angle between the brush and paper is not necessarily an exact right angle. Use your thumb and all the fingers to hold the brush, with the thumb pressing on one side of the brush shaft, the forefinger holding back, the middle finger reinforcing the forefinger, the ring finger pushing the brush shaft and the little finger reinforcing the ring finger. Leave an empty "cave" in your palm. You should not hold the brush with a fist!

Your wrist works too

When you write, not only your fingers work, but your wrist should move as well. There are three ways of using the wrist. If you write small characters, your right wrist may rest on the table, or maybe you wish to support the right wrist with the left hand.

The right wrist rests on the table. Photograph by Wen Jingen

When you write 5-10 cm large characters, you must raise your right wrist from the table, but your right elbow may rest on the table. This will enable your hand to move in a larger motion.

The right wrist is raised above the table. Photograph by Wen Jingen

When you write still larger characters or write on a large sheet of paper, raise your elbow above the table. Thus your right arm can move within a larger diameter and ensure a good control of the brush.

The right elbow is raised above the table. Photograph by Wen Jingen

When you write, be sure that your wrist is not strained. The brush should not be held too tightly; otherwise the movement of the hand (and of the brush) will be hampered.

It takes time to master these ways of holding the brush.

Tracing and Copying Model Calligraphic Works

Rubbings and copybooks

Chinese calligraphic works are mostly executed with black ink on white paper. Many books of model calligraphy have white characters against a black ground — this is because those copybooks are rubbings from stones. Some masterpieces were originally stone inscriptions and they have been handed down in the form of rubbings. Other calligraphic masterpieces were done on paper. In ancient China, when the printing technology was not sophisticated enough to reproduce art works, people transferred calligraphic works onto stones and made rubbings from them to distribute those masterpieces. It goes without saying that you will write your characters in ink when you copy characters from the rubbing-based copybooks.

Sometimes, both the original calligraphic work on paper and its stone rubbings have survived, providing us with a good opportunity for comparing them and seeing the authentic look of ancient calligraphic works.

Lingfei Canon attributed to Zhong Shaojing
(d. AD 746), original on paper

Lingfei Canon attributed to Zhong Shaojing,
rubbing from stone

Tracing and copying model calligraphic works is a must for beginners of Chinese calligraphy. There are several ways of tracing model characters from a copybook.

In the past people used to print master sheets of calligraphy in red ink. Students covered the red strokes with their black ink marks. This method can be used during the initial stage of study.

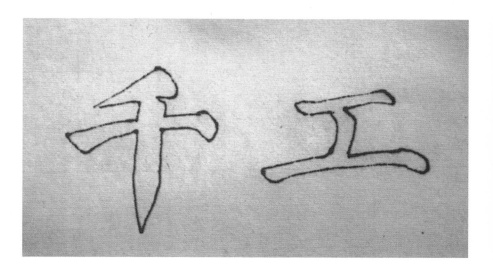

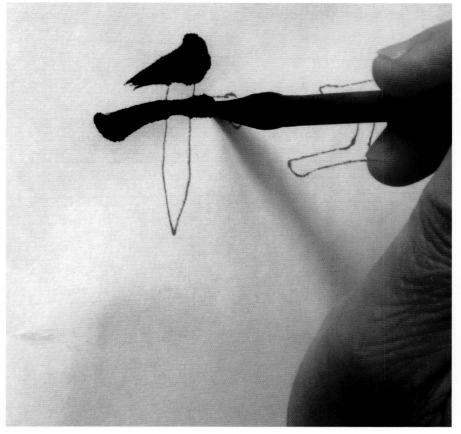

Illustrations by Wen Jingen

Another way was to cover the copybook with a sheet of transparent paper and trace the model characters underneath with ink. You must trace in a "stroke for stroke" method and not be tempted to retouch your stroke. Do not trace the contour of a character from the copybook and then fill in the outlines in the way you colour a colouring book (unless you mean to make an exact replica of the original piece rather than to study calligraphy).

Some people trace the outline of the model characters and then fill the contours with ink. In that case, you must complete a stroke "at one go". In other word, the contour of one stroke must be filled by your *one* stroke.

Copying model calligraphic works is the next step of learning. This procedure has three stages.

At the first stage, the student has a copybook at his or her side. Do not copy single characters *stroke by stroke*. A character produced this way lacks coherence. Instead, copy the master sheet *character by character*. You should scrutinise one character in the copybook for a while and then write this character in one go. If the result is not to your liking, write it once more. When you are experienced in copying a master sheet character by character, you may try to copy it line by line.

During the next stage you may try to copy model characters from your memory. Do not look at the copybook when you write. After you have written one or two pages, open the copybook and compare it with your writing. Repeat this until your characters resemble those in the copybook.

For the final stage, you may "copy" a copybook with your own innovation. You reproduce the style and charm of the copybook but you can also write characters that are not found in the copybook — yet these characters should be in the style of the model characters in the book. To achieve this, you must have a sound training and conceive your writing well before you put the brush on the paper. This is a preparatory stage to independent calligraphic creation.

The style of calligraphy is related to the writer's personal character, temperament, literary or artistic taste and outlook on world. When you choose a calligrapher as a model, try to find one whose style is to your taste.

There are thousands of Chinese characters. It is not necessary or possible for you to write them all. When you choose characters to copy, choose those whose structural features are representative. For example, if you learn to write 地 where the left radical 土 is smaller than the right radical and the last stroke rises up towards the right radical, it will be easy for you to write similar characters like 埋, 坏 and 坦.

It is better to write a few characters repeatedly than writing many characters at one sitting i.e. repeat 5 characters 30 times each in half an hour, rather than writing 150 different characters.

When you practise calligraphy from a master sheet, you must force yourself to follow the models. If you write in your own usual way, the model characters are useless. At first, your writing may be quite different from that in the copybook. Stick at it; try to correct your faulty strokes and structures to bring your characters as close to the model as possible. Keep on doing this and you will make constant progress.

Why is your handwriting always different from the model characters?

Copying model characters from copybooks has been proven as an efficient learning method. The student should model his or her handwriting on the characters in the copybooks. By this exercise you will by and by correct your bad writing habits and make progress. But you will find that however hard you work on the master sheet, your handwriting is not exactly the same as the model characters. This is quite natural. One's handwriting is like one's disposition — it is obstinate and cannot be hidden.

The following picture shows a line from Liu Gongquan's calligraphic work.

The following is a copy done by the celebrated calligrapher Huang Ziyuan (1873 — 1918)

Compare the stroke at the arrows and the corresponding stroke in the picture below. You will see that Huang's copy reveals his own style — slimmer and less full strokes.

Characters from Huang Ziyuan's another calligraphic work

Brushwork

The stroke is the basic element of Chinese calligraphy. To produce a good stroke, you must control your brush and move it according to certain principles.

A stroke has a beginning, a centre movement and an end. In this manual, to illustrate the execution of a stroke, the track of the movement of the brush tip is marked with a line within the outline of a stroke.

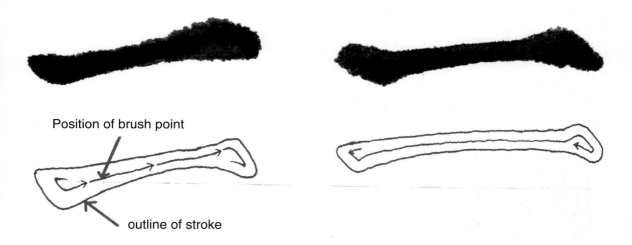

Position of brush point

outline of stroke

When you wield your brush to make a stroke, you must pay attention to three aspects of it. They are:

1. You apply different pressures to your brush. Variation of pressure helps to avoid dull and monotonous strokes.

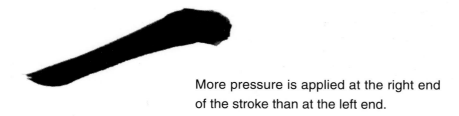

More pressure is applied at the right end of the stroke than at the left end.

2. The speed of the brush movement may vary within a stroke or in different strokes in one character.

However, too fast or too slow brushwork is not desirable. Too fast brushwork looks flimsy. Too slow brushwork tends to be clumsy.

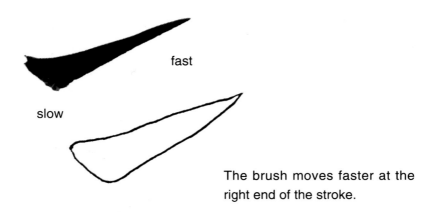

fast

slow

The brush moves faster at the right end of the stroke.

3. The brush may be lifted and pressed during its movement. When the brush is lifted, the stroke produced becomes thinner. When it is pressed, the stroke produced is thicker.

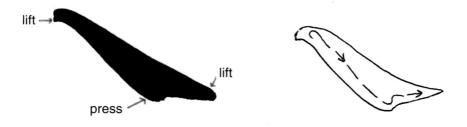

lift →

lift

press

The brush is lifted at the top of the stroke, pressed as it approaches the "heel" and finally lifted off at the end.

The position of the point of the brush tip and various strokes

The point of the brush tip may be exposed.

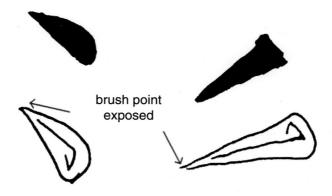

brush point
exposed

It may also be concealed within the stroke. Such a stroke appears full and vigorous.

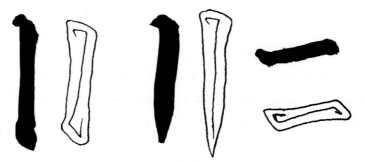

If the brush tip is kept at the centre of the stroke, the stroke is called "centre-tip stroke". A centre-tip stroke looks full and sturdy.

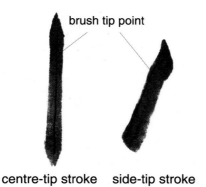

brush tip point

centre-tip stroke   side-tip stroke

Centre-tip and side-tip strokes.
Illustration by Wen Jingen

On the other hand, if the brush tip is kept to one side of the stroke, this is a "side-tip stroke". Side-tip strokes are seldom used in calligraphy.

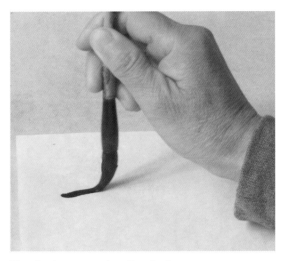 

Producing a centre-tip stroke.

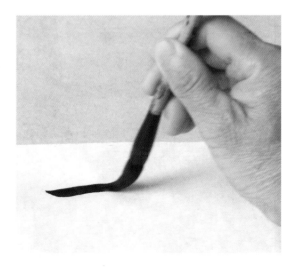

Producing a side-tip stroke. Illustrations by Wen Jingen

Sometimes you may "cut in" a stroke. If you mean to produce a horizontal stroke, you start the stroke by laying the brush tip down vertically. If you mean to produce a vertical stroke, you start the stroke by laying the brush tip down horizontally.

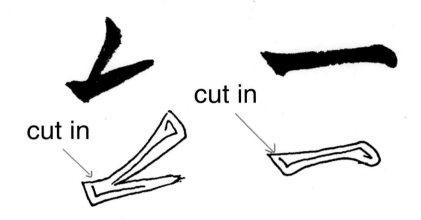

cut in

cut in

Absolutely straight strokes are not desirable. Ancient Chinese calligraphers tried to achieve some "curving" within the lines that are straight on the whole. This adds liveliness to the strokes.

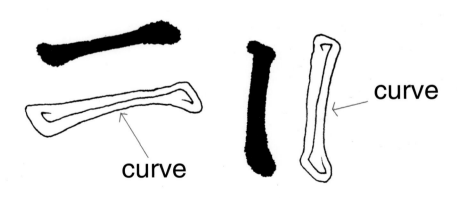

curve

curve

Also, sometimes a stroke may "break" at a point. It may break completely or just slightly.

Note that the brush is pressed onto or raised from the paper at certain points of a stroke. A turning may be angular or round.

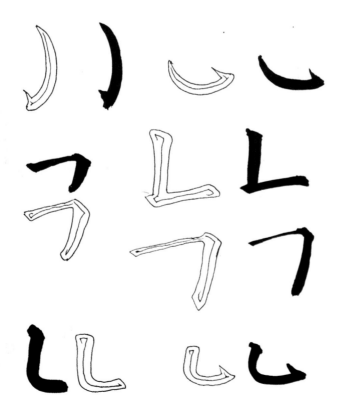

Sequence of Strokes in a Character

In this manual, the sequence of strokes is indicated by numbers marked at the beginning of a stroke, when necessary.

Illustration by Wen Jingen

Here are some principles governing the sequence of strokes in regular calligraphy:

1. from left to right;   2. from top to bottom;

3. horizontal before vertical;   4. left-falling before right falling;

5. bottom last;

6. closing the "gate" after everything has entered the "house";

7. an open frame on top, reversed L-shaped frame on the left shoulder or right shoulder first;

8. basin-shaped or L-shaped frame on bottom last;

9. the middle, tall vertical first;

10. single dots on right side or right shoulder last;

11. the left L-shaped turning before the right one;

Certain characters have special sequences of strokes:

These principles are not invariable. Strokes in some characters may be written in different sequence. Example, 方

In certain cases, calligraphers like to alternate vertical and horizontal strokes. This may account for different sequences of the same radical. For example, in the character 有 the first stroke is the left falling stroke, the second horizontal and the third stroke is vertical. So the first strokes are top-down, horizontal and top-down again. While in the character 左, the first stroke is the horizontal one. The first strokes are horizontal, top-down and then horizontal again.

Basic Strokes

There are eight basic strokes. They are: the dot (*dian* 点[點]), horizontal (*heng* 横), vertical (*shu* 竖[竪]), left falling (*pie* 撇), right falling (*na* 捺), rising (*ti* 提), turning (*zhe* 折) and hook strokes (*gou* 钩[鈎]).

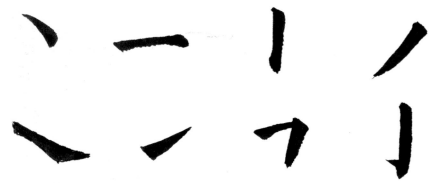

(1) **Dot.** The dot stroke may take on different shapes. It is not easy to produce a good dot. Attention must be paid to the beginning and the end of the stroke. Sometimes the path of the brush tip is concealed and in other times it is exposed.

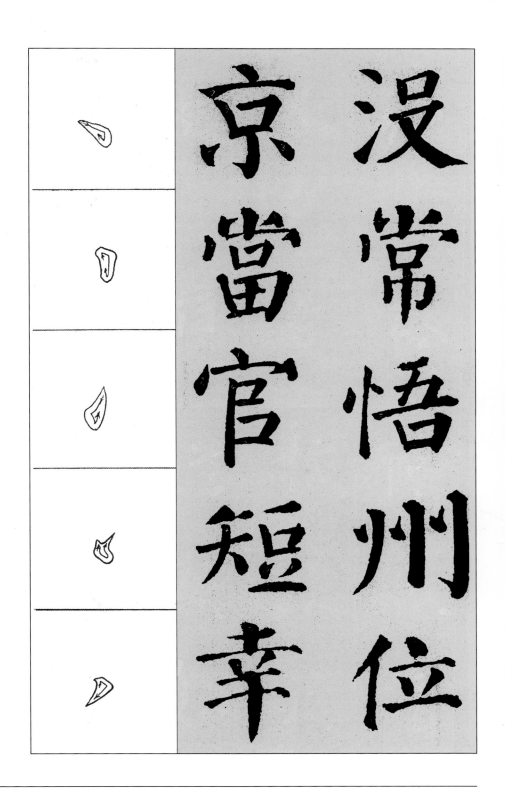

没常悟州位

京當官短幸

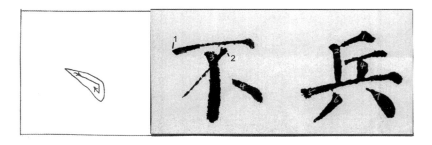

(2) **Horizontal stroke.**

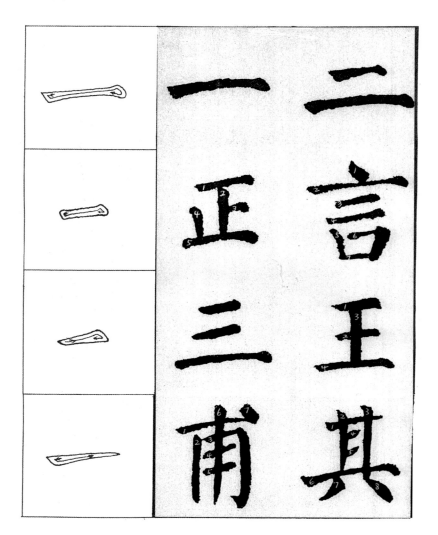

Chinese Regular Script Calligraphy for Beginners

(3) **Vertical stroke.** Some verticals have a sharp end — the point of the brush tip is exposed at its lower end. Some vertical strokes have a blunt end — the brush tip is concealed within the stroke. The vertical stroke is not always absolutely vertical, sometimes it may be slight curved.

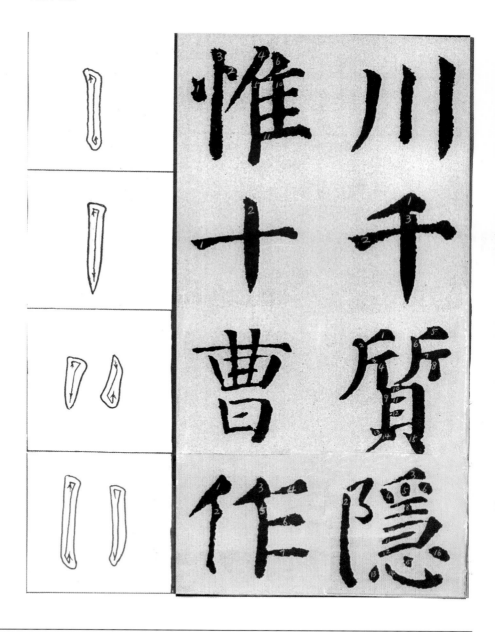

(4) **Left falling stroke.** Again, you must note how a stroke is started, how the brush tip moves along and how the stroke is finished.

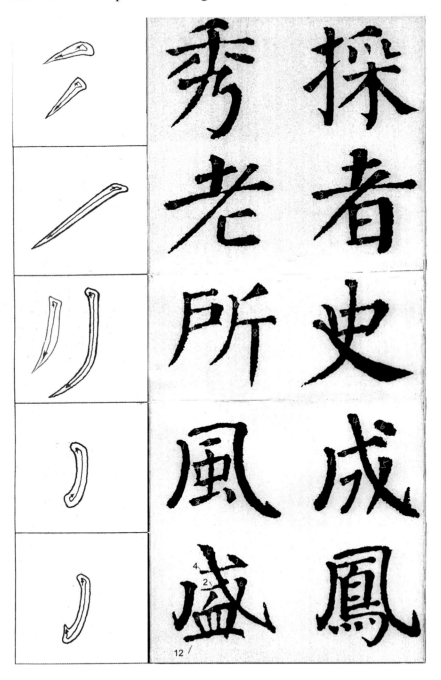

(5) **Right falling stroke.** This stroke has a wavy movement of the brush tip. Before it is completed, the brush is pressed and then lifted.

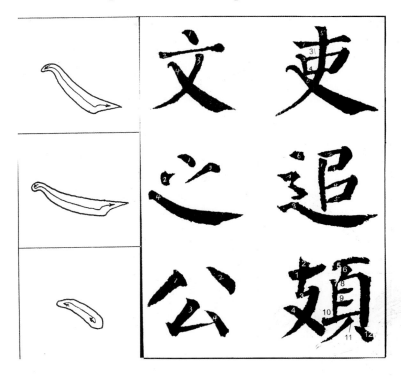

(6) **Rising stroke.** This stroke looks like a sword. It may be at 45° or less.

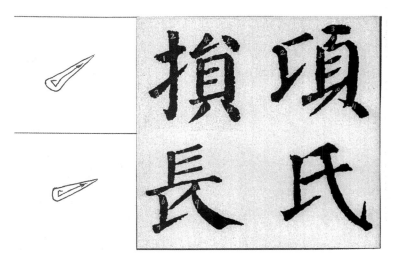

(7) **Turning stroke.** Some turning strokes are at a sharp angle, while others are rounded. Some turning strokes may look broken.

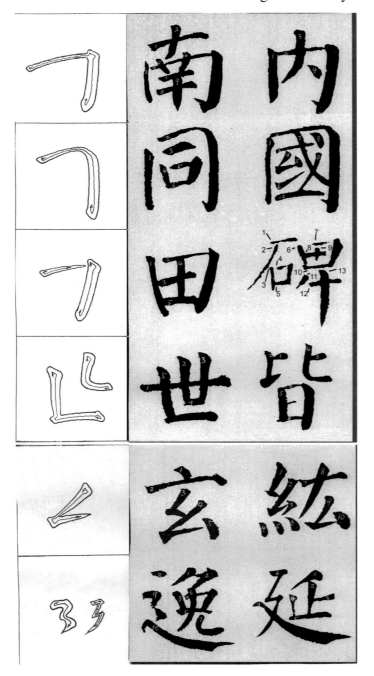

(8) **Hook.** This kind of stroke has many variations. An important feature of the hook stroke is its end. A hook with a well-executed tail looks beautiful.

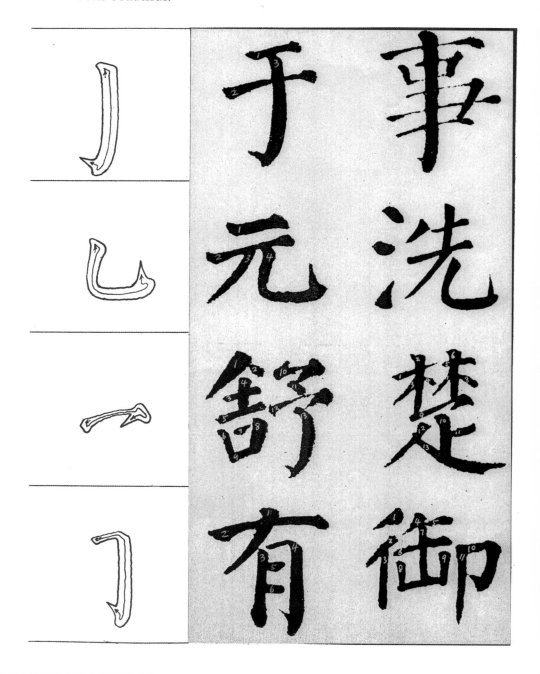

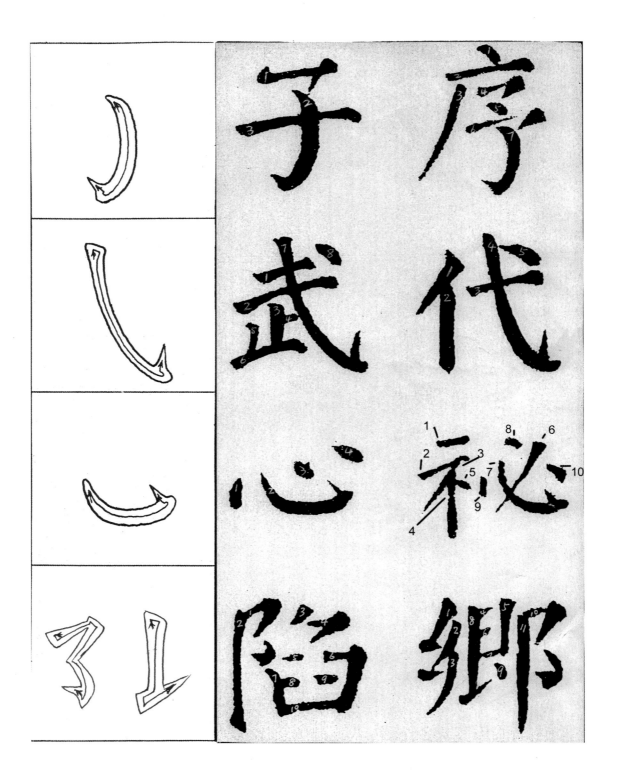

Chinese Regular Script Calligraphy for Beginners

The Structure

Nearly 37% of Chinese characters are inseparable blocks. The other 63% consist of two or more radicals in left-right, top-down, or inner-and-outer structures.

Block characters: 人 十 申 垂

Characters with two or more components:

Left-right:

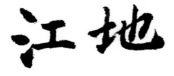

Left-centre-right:

Top-bottom:

思 呂

Top-middle-bottom:

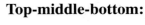

Encircled:

Half-encircled:

臣 司 同 厚 逢 幽

Multiple-structure:

霜 笑 提 剖 席

厢 迢 逛 间 阀

Illustrations by Wen Jingen

The various shapes of Chinese characters fall into the following types:

Large square block:

Small square block:

Upright rectangle

Horizontal rectangle

Left tilting:

Right tilting:

Top narrow:

Top wide:

Top wide:

Left short:

Right short:

Diamond:

Arrange the basic strokes with skill

To achieve a beautiful structure, the basic strokes must be arranged skilfully. Here are some enlightening examples:

In the character 悟, the left radical has two dots. The left dot is long and the right one short. The left dot is upright and the right one sloping. This variation of size and position makes the radical gracefully uneven. The character 於 has three dots. The dot in the upper left part is near the horizontal stroke underneath it. The two dots on the right are farther from the top radical 人. As a result, strokes in both the left radical and the right radical are largely equally spaced.

If the dots are executed otherwise, the characters have unbalanced structures. Illustration by Wen Jingen

The first stroke in the character 小 is the vertical stroke in the middle. It ends with a hook pointing to the left dot. The two dots are at a level corresponding to the middle part of the vertical stroke. The left dot has its end pointing to the top of the right dot. The three strokes form a coherent whole. The top of the character 光 is a 小. The left dot points to the right and the right dot points to the left. The two dots echo each other.

Otherwise they lack coherence. Illustration by Wen Jingen

Usually dots on the top and in the middle part are small and dots at the bottom and on the sides are larger.

All these characters have dots. They take on a different shape to fit into different structures.

All these characters have horizontal strokes. The horizontal strokes in the character 言 are long and they are equally spaced. The horizontal stroke in the character 氏 is slightly tilted. It has a 20° angle with the horizontal to suit the left falling stroke above it. The horizontal strokes in 也 and 九 are slanting too, because these two characters have a long turning stroke.

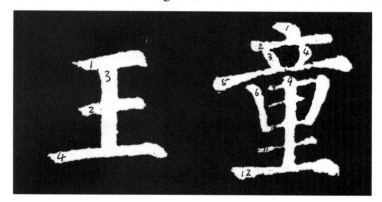

Each of these characters has several horizontal strokes. They should be of different lengths. The longer horizontal strokes have a slight curve in their middle part, and the shorter ones are straighter.

In these two characters, the horizontal strokes within the frame at the centre join the left vertical stroke but do not join the right of the frame. This gives the central part of the character more breathing space.

Compare:

Illustration by Wen Jingen

The vertical stroke in these four characters is treated in a different way. The lower half is sharp (with the brush tip exposed) in 十, blunt (with the brush tip concealed) in 不, and oblique in 土 and 五. If the vertical stroke in 不 has a sharp end, the top of the character will appear too heavy for the bottom. If the vertical strokes in 五 are upright, the whole character will look rigid.

Otherwise, they appear too stiff. Illustration by Wen Jingen

When parallel vertical strokes appear in a character, one of them (usually the left one) has a blunt end while the others have a sharp one.

If a character has two parallel vertical strokes, the right one is higher than the left one.

Otherwise, they are unsteady. Illustration by Wen Jingen

Two vertical strokes as parts of a frame are at different heights. Usually, the left one is shorter than the right one. Otherwise the whole character looks unsteady, as shown below.

Illustration by Wen Jingen

Note the left-falling strokes in these characters are of different lengths and at different angles. 度 has two left-falling strokes. The outer one is longer and straighter than the inner one. In the character 秀 the three left-falling strokes are of different lengths and angles.

If the left-falling strokes are arranged parallel, the whole character has an awkward posture. Illustration by Wen Jingen

Each of these characters has two right-falling strokes. To avoid monotony, one of them (the last stroke in the lower radical of 秦 and the last stroke of the left radical of 林) take on the form of dots.

Otherwise the result will be unsightly. Illustration by Wen Jingen

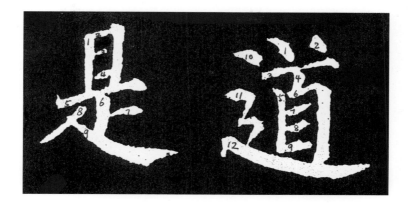

The right-falling stroke at the bottom of a character should be long enough to support the whole character.

If the right-falling stroke at the bottom of a character is not long enough, the whole character appears to have too small a base. Illustration by Wen Jingen

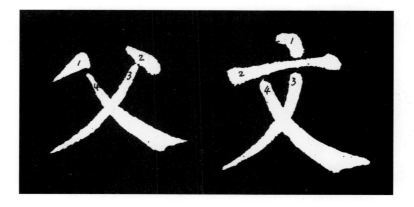

The left-falling and right-falling strokes often cross each other at the centre of the character.

If the two slanting strokes do not cross at the centre of the character, the overall character looks unbalanced. Illustration by Wen Jingen

In these characters, the left-falling and right-falling strokes are roughly symmetrical.

If they are not symmetrical, the whole character is out of balance. Illustration by Wen Jingen

The rising stroke in 公 is flat because it is at the bottom of the character. The rising stroke in 氏 is steeper; otherwise the space at the centre would be too large. Therefore the result will be like this.

Illustration by Wen Jingen

In these two characters, a stroke of the right radical thrusts into the space in the left radical. At the same time, the left and right radical do not collide with each other. The whole structure is compact and harmonious.

Otherwise the whole character looks too loose. Illustration by Wen Jingen

When two turning strokes appear in one character or one turning stroke has two turns, the turning stroke on the top takes on a square form and the turning stroke at the bottom is round.

Otherwise they are unsightly. Illustration by Wen Jingen

The brush may be raised at the turning of a stroke as shown in the character 月, but the raised part must not be too high. Also, the stroke may droop at the turning point as shown in the character 日, but it must not be too drastic.

Otherwise the turning stroke looks weak or clumsy. Illustration by Wen Jingen

A left-hook is usually short and a right-hook is long. The left-hook in the character 于 has no strokes around it; if its end extends too far, the left half of the character is heavier than the right and thus the whole character is out of balance. In the character 以 there is a large blank space at the top of the left radical. If the left-vertical hook has a short tail, the blank space will appear too empty.

Illustration by Wen Jingen

If the hook in 于 is large and the hook in 以 is small, the result will look uncomfortable.

If a hook points outward, it should be large. If a hook points to the centre of the character, it should be small, as in the right hand character. The characters on the right look uncomfortable because their hooks are out of proportion.

When two or more hook strokes appear in one character, try to write them in different ways. The character 簿 may have two hooks. One hook is omitted. The character 沈 has two hooks. The top hook is smaller than the bottom one.

Otherwise, the characters are in an uncomfortable posture.
Illustration by Wen Jingen

The right radical of the character 部 and the left radical of the character 陆 are the same 阝. But they are written in different sizes. The radical in the left character points outward, so it is large. In the right character, it points to the inner part of the character, so it must give way to the right hand side.

If the right 阝 is large and the left one is small, the whole structure is out of balance. Illustration by Wen Jingen

Pages for You to Copy

You have now learned some principles on the good structure of characters. There may be more guidelines for you to study, but on the whole Chinese calligraphy is a visual art and not a science. So what really matters is your intuitive comprehension which can only be achieved through seeing and doing. Here are some pages for you to copy. They are taken from Yan Zhenqing's inscription of a *Qin Li Bei* 勤礼[禮]碑 stele. If you have an interest in his calligraphy, you may buy his copybooks in China's bookshops. If you copy other calligraphers' works, the calligraphic styles may differ, but the principles governing the writing of various strokes and forming a good structure are more or less the same.

Chinese Regular Script Calligraphy for Beginners

質	曾	晚
貽	旦	暮
贈	水	書
見	泉	曹

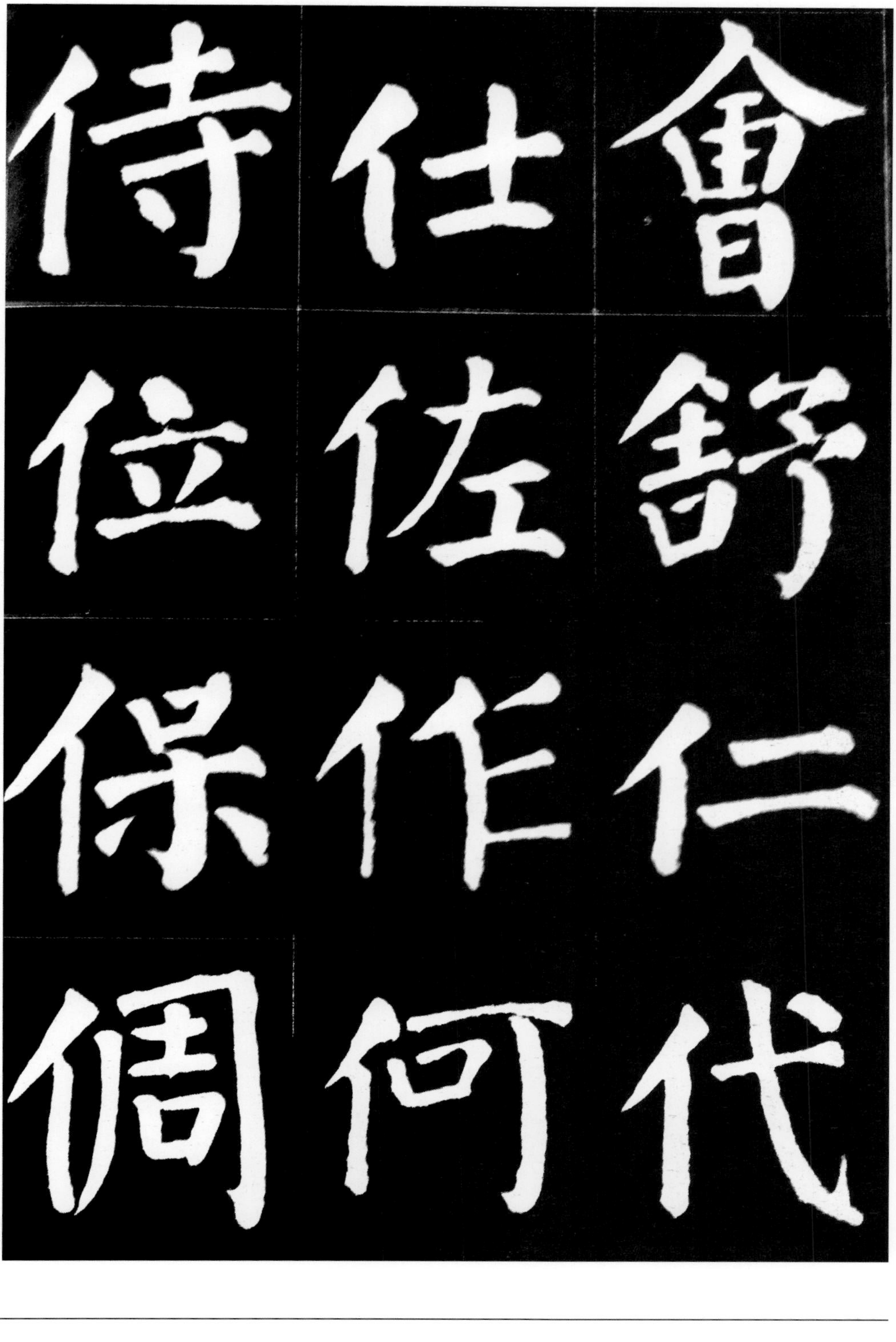
會舒仁代
仕佐作何
侍位保倜

業 柳 理
戌 相 班
武 杭 李
威 集 林

國 田 同 四

唐 司 威 道

度 威 過

司 周 山

旭 臣 圖

Traditional and simplified Chinese characters

In olden times, many Chinese characters had variations. Because Chinese characters are not easy to memorise, people tended to write the same characters in different ways. Some variations were evidently simpler than the others. Efforts were made to unify the forms of Chinese writing with little success. In 1956 the government of the People's Republic of China made a number of simplified characters as the standard. Since then simplified characters have been used in all publications. Traditional forms are still used, mainly in historical documents. They are also used in China's Taiwan Province, Hong Kong and Macao special administrative regions. Many calligraphers like to write the traditional characters because those are what they copy from ancient copybooks when they study calligraphy. But it is absolutely wrong to say traditional characters are more beautiful than the simplified ones. Well-written simplified Chinese characters are no less beautiful than traditional ones. The beauty of calligraphy lies in your artistic cultivation.

Illustration by Wen Jingen

Specimens of traditional and simplified Chinese characters:

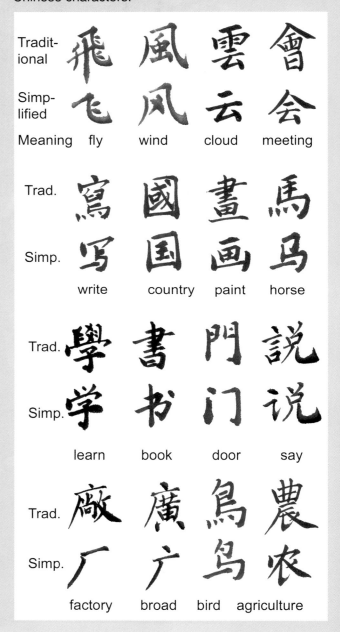

Traditional	飛	風	雲	會
Simplified	飞	凤	云	会
Meaning	fly	wind	cloud	meeting
Trad.	寫	國	畫	馬
Simp.	写	国	画	马
	write	country	paint	horse
Trad.	學	書	門	説
Simp.	学	书	门	说
	learn	book	door	say
Trad.	廠	廣	鳥	農
Simp.	厂	广	鸟	农
	factory	broad	bird	agriculture

Composition

To arrange characters beautifully on a sheet of paper, you must first of all consider the format of your writing. There are several traditional formats. The whole sheet of paper hanging on the wall of a salon or sitting room is called *zhongtang* 中堂 (literally, "at centre of a hall"). A narrow scroll is called *tiaofu* 条[條]幅 ("narrow sheet"). A set of four, six or eight or even ten long hanging scrolls side by side is called *ping* 屏 ("screen"). A horizontal sheet of paper is called *hengfu* 横幅 ("horizontal sheet"). The panel over the gate to a building is usually in horizontal format. A hanging couplet *duizi* 对[對]子 or *duilian* 对联 [對聯] often hangs on the wall of a salon, sometimes on both sides of a *zhongtang*, on door flaps, or on both side pillars of a stage. Calligraphic works can also be created on album leaves or a fan. The hand scroll *shoujuan* 手卷 is a very long (sometimes tens of metres) horizontal scroll.

Hanging scroll written by Weng Tonghe (1830—1904)

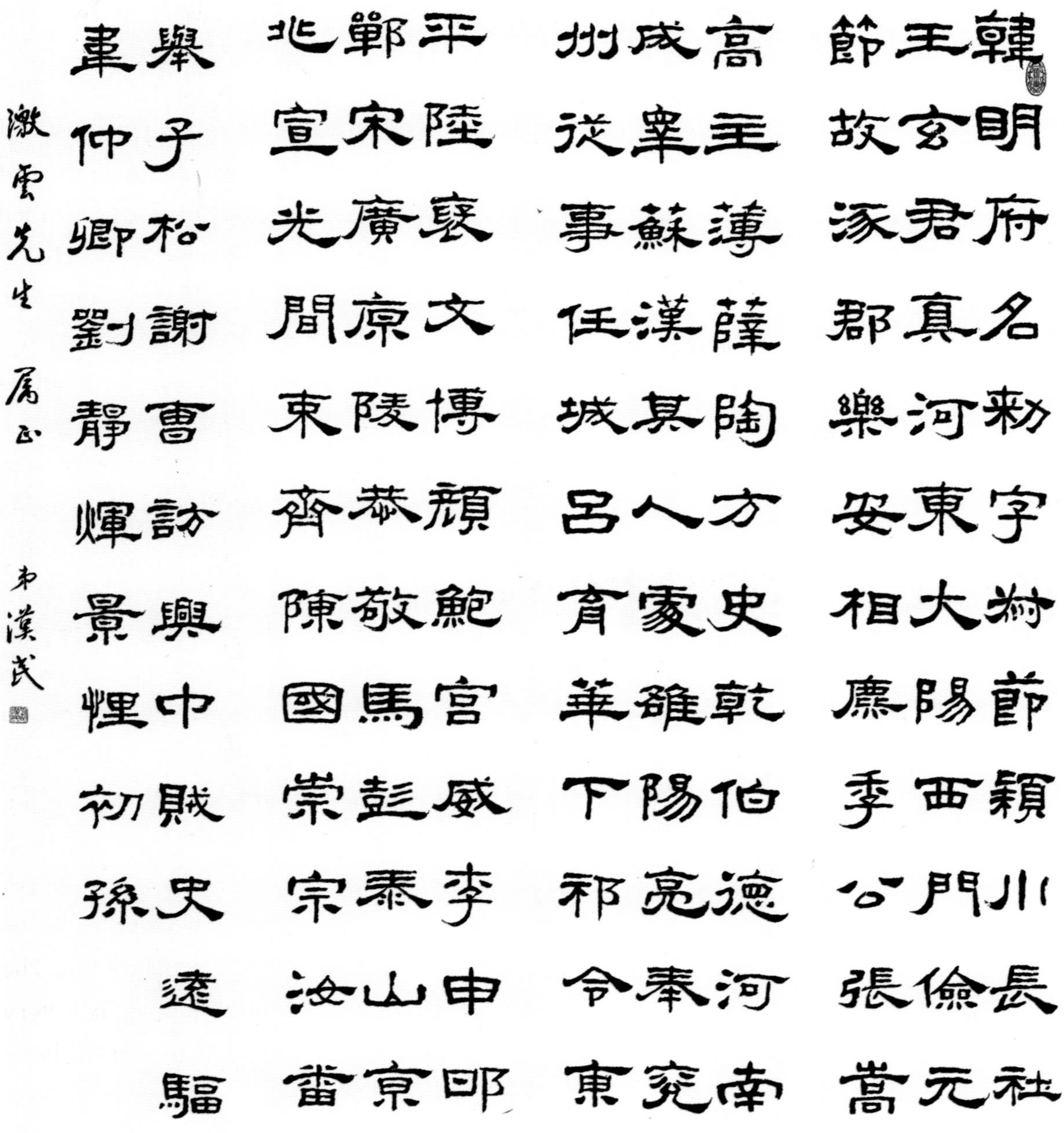

韓明府名莿字樹節潁川長社
王故涿郡名真河東大陽西門倫元嵩
高主薛薄陶方史乾伯德河南兗
成羣蘇漢其人豪雛陽亮奉東
平陸襃文博顏鮑宮威李申邨
邯鄲宋廣原陵恭敬馬彭黍山京邑
兆宣光間束齊陳國崇宗汾雷
舉子松謝曹訪與中賊史遠騙
車仲卿劉靜輝景煇初孫

漱雪先生屬正
胡漢民

Set of four screens written by Hu Hanmin (1879 — 1936)

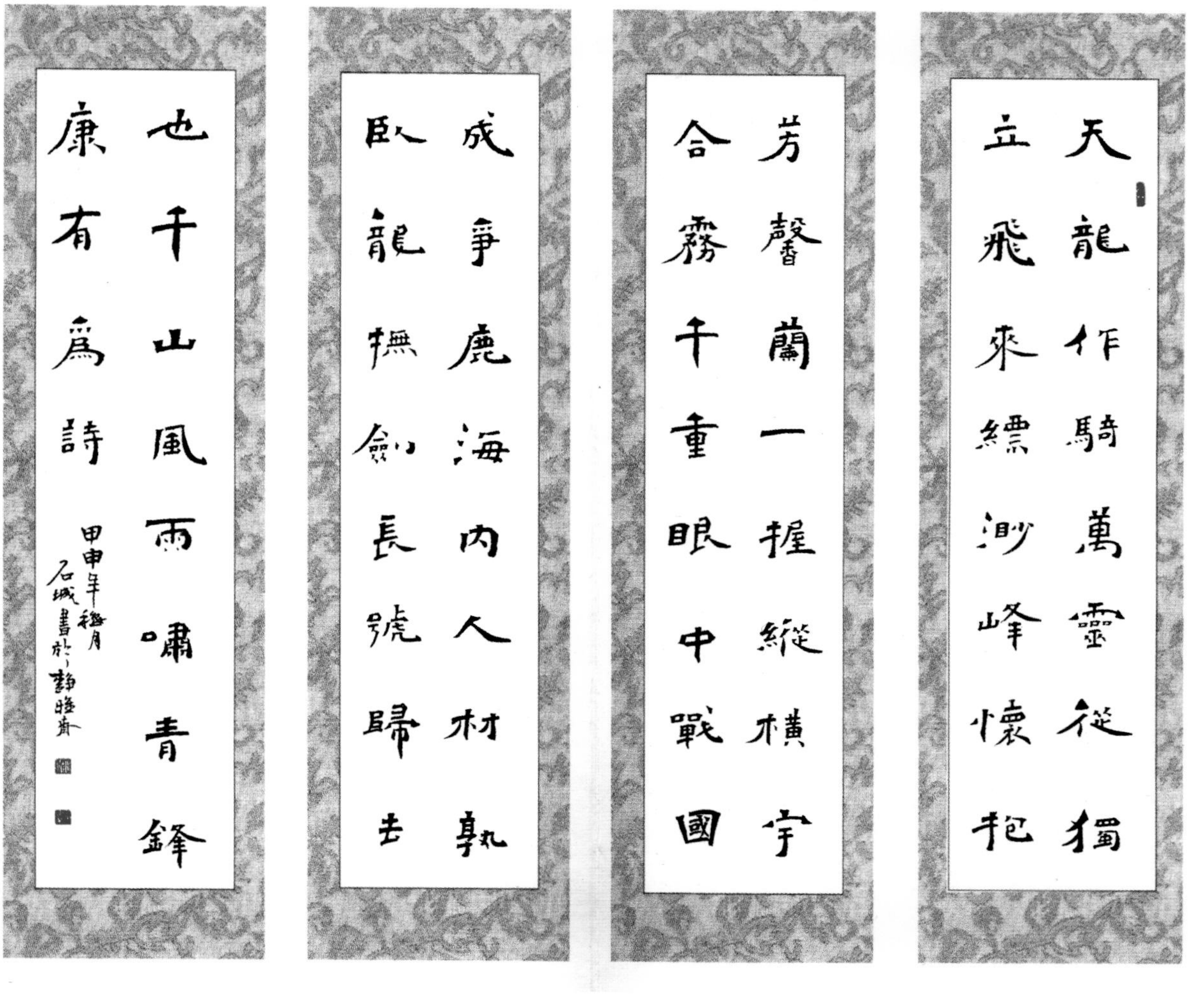

天龍作騎萬靈從獨
立飛來縹渺峰懷抱

芳馨蘭一握縱橫宇
合霧千重眼中戰國

成爭鹿海內人材亟
臥龍撫劍長號歸去

也千山風雨嘯青鋒
鋒
康有爲詩
甲申年穀月
石城書於靜怡齋

Hanging couplet written by Li Ruiqing
(1867-1920)

Fan with calligraphy of Dong Gao (1740-1818)

To compose a beautiful calligraphic work, you must have a good arrangement of the distances between strokes and characters, among lines and the width of margins. Usually, the top and bottom margins can be 5 to 10 centimetres wide and the left and right margins can be 3 to 6 centimetres.

To arrange your characters evenly, you can fold your paper in two directions to produce grids and write one character in each square. When the work is finished and mounted, the folded grids will disappear.

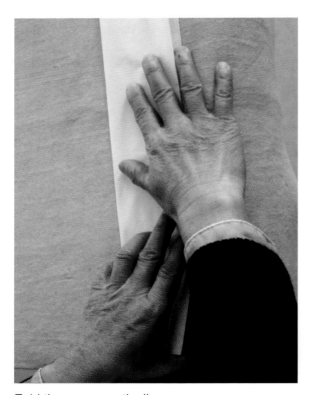

Fold the paper vertically

Fold the paper horizontally

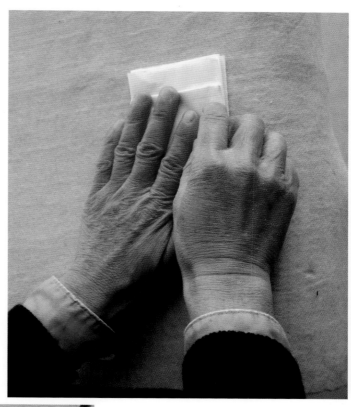

Illustrations by Wen Jingen

You can also draw grids in red ink. Some calligraphers draw the grids with a pencil and when the work is completed, they erase the pencil grids with a rubber — do take care not to harm the paper if you try this. Some calligraphers fold the paper to mark vertical lines but do not use the horizontal folds. When they write on a sheet of paper processed this way, each line of characters is written between two folds but horizontally, the characters are random.

Traditionally, the first line is not indented. Most Chinese calligraphers observe the convention of not using punctuation marks. If the last line has too few characters, it appears empty. But if it has too many characters, the whole piece looks stuffy.

Chinese calligraphers like putting their colophon at the end of a calligraphic work. A colophon may contain the writer's name plus a date only or a comment concerning the motivation of the creation of the calligraphic work. An often seen commentary is "written by order of Mr./Ms./Professor..." (xxx 先生／女士／教授……嘱) or "to be rectified by Mr./Ms./Professor..." (xxx 先生／女士／教授……教正／指正／雅正)

Most Chinese calligraphers use one or more seal imprints, often to the left of the colophon, on their calligraphy. The legend of a seal may be a person's name. The meaning of a so-called "leisure seal" *xianzhang* 闲[閑]章 may be a comment, a maxim, an adage, or a line from a poem. If you would like to follow suit, you can impress your seals on your calligraphic work too. The seal impression, however, is not absolutely necessary for all calligraphers.

Seals and seal paste, photograph by Sun Shuming

Conceiving and Execution

Before you put your brush on the paper, conceive your creation carefully. You should consider what you will write, what a format you will adopt, sizes of paper (or other material) and characters, the distance between lines and characters etc., what colophon you will add to the work, and the seals you wish to impress on it. Only with all these questions answered in your head, can you create a successful piece of calligraphy.

In execution you must pay attention to the following matters.

First of all, the initial character is very important. It determines the size, thickness of strokes and the style of all the other characters on the paper.

Secondly, the size of all characters should be more or less the same. If a character has many strokes, the strokes should be thin and the structure should be compact. If a character has few strokes, the strokes should be thick and the structure should be open.

Thirdly, you may write traditional characters and you may also write simplified characters. But it is better not to mix them in one piece of calligraphy.

Finally, the ink shade must also be uniform through the whole piece.

Hang up your work

When you finish a calligraphic work, hang it up on the wall. Once a piece of calligraphy is hung, it is easy for you to discover faulty strokes, characters and any errors in the composition. Once you find your faults, you can then try to correct them next time you write those characters.

More Model Calligraphic Works

1. Inscription on Yuan Lüe's tombstone 元略墓志 written by an unknown calligrapher in AD 528, in "Northern-Wei Stele" style

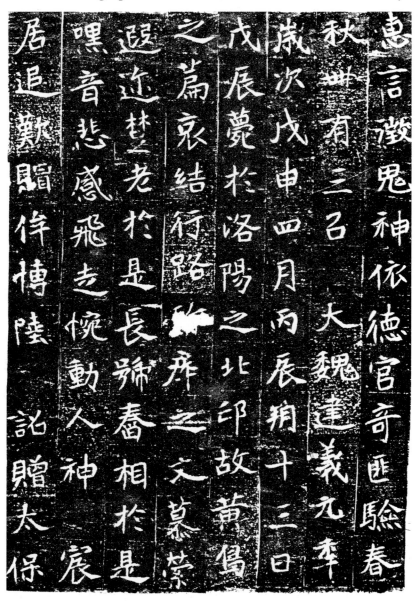

魏故持中驃騎大將軍儀同三

司尚書令徐州刾史太保東平

王元君墓誌銘

君諱略字攜興司州河南洛陽

都鄉照交里人也大魏景穆

皇帝之曾孫南安惠王之孫司

徒公中山獻武王之第四子源

資氣始号曰物初高祖深鏡

品族洞曉宗由窮万隙之本則

大易氏君高朗幼樹令問風遠

之楨排山川而獨頴遊志儒林

如辟之損豪琳琅以先奇維國

宅心仁苑禮窮訓則義周物軌

信等脫鯣惠誅贈綍器博宏致

筆茂子雲汪汪焉量溢万頃濟

濟焉實懷多士世宗宣武皇

徐州刺史謚曰玄貞王窆窆于

洛城之西陵夫皇周紀易循環

莫息泉靈綿代或穨戎後故樹

鐫琢之文永題不朽之石其詞

尊

維天梃氣維嶽降靈狥與顯垢

資和詑形學由心曉眉召性成

辟強幼達令思早名彼一此

2. Inscription on Duke Zheng's tombstone (*Zheng Wengong bei* 郑[鄭]文公碑) AD 551, written by Zheng Zhaodao, in the "Northern-Wei Stele" style

軍事史南
尭安公陽
州東鄭
刾将君文
之

人也肇洪
源於有周
幼驎司州
燊陽開封

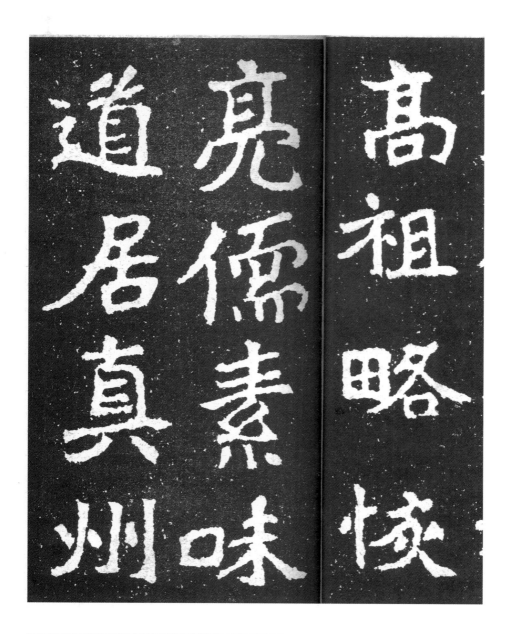

貞公祖溫常鄉濟南中山尹太

六十有七寢疾薨於位凡百君子莫不悲

薄東郡程
天賜菁六
十人仰道

3. Inscription on Hermit Wang's Brick Pagoda Tomb 王居士砖[磚]塔铭[銘] written by Jing Ke, AD 658

昌辭冠後嘅樂府歌

其載德天下挹其家

不刊介石就播微猷

吁其嗟焉乃為銘曰

懿矣居士明我悟真

幽鑒彼岸妙道問津

苦節無撓貞心刻勤
顧邈三有超俯十輪
俄隨惲化邊此遷神
歸然靈塔長欽後人

原晉陽之也英宗頻
邁遠胄隆周後緒遐

4. "On Sweet Spring at Jiucheng Palace" written by Ouyang Xun (AD 557 — 641) 九成宫醴泉铭[銘]

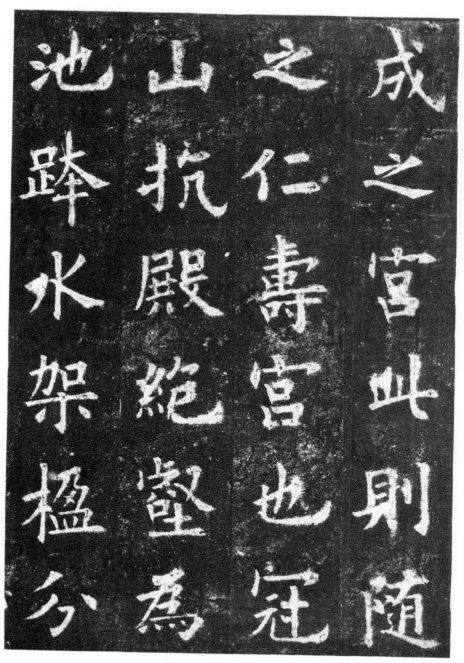

之膝地漢之甘
泉不能尚也
皇帝爰在弱冠
經營四方逮乎

立年撫臨億兆始以武功壹海內終以文德懷遠人束越青丘

明聖既可蠲兹

沈痼又將延彼

遐齡是以百辟

卿士相趍動色

5. "Warrant (certificate for Yan's official appointment) for Yan Zhenqing in the hand of Yan Zhenqing" (AD 709—785) 颜[顏]真卿自书[書]告身帖

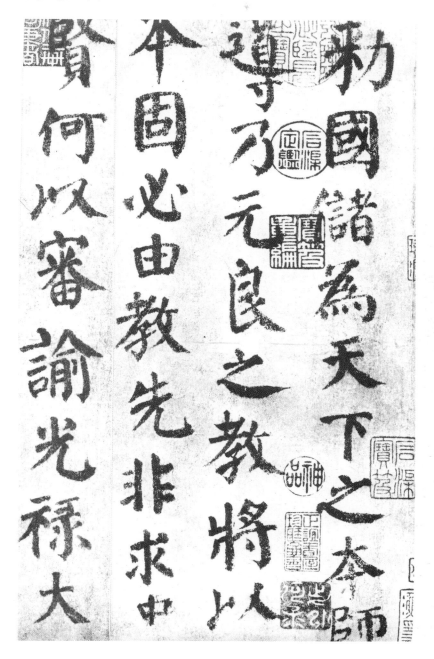

夫行吏部尚書克禮
儀使上柱國魯郡開
國公顏真卿立德
踐行當四科之首談

其直方動用謂之縣

解山公啓事清彼品

流州孫制禮光我王

度惟是一有寶貢萬

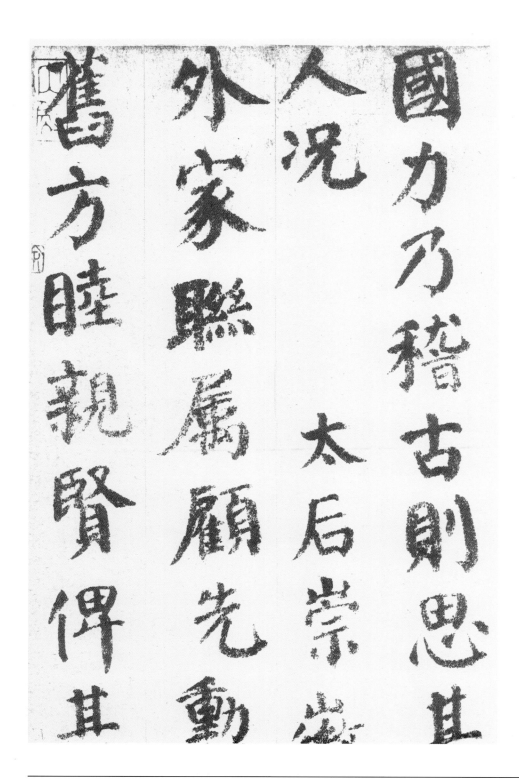

國力乃稽古則思甚
人況　太后崇巂
外家隸屬顧先動
舊方睦親賢俾其

6. "Inscription on the Shence Army Stele" written by Liu Gongquan (AD 778 —865) 神策军[軍]碑

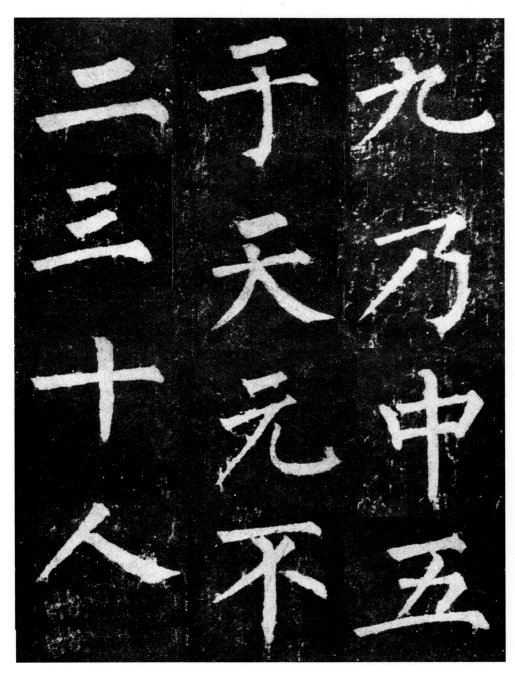

丹常来事
果相集森
心恩忘慰

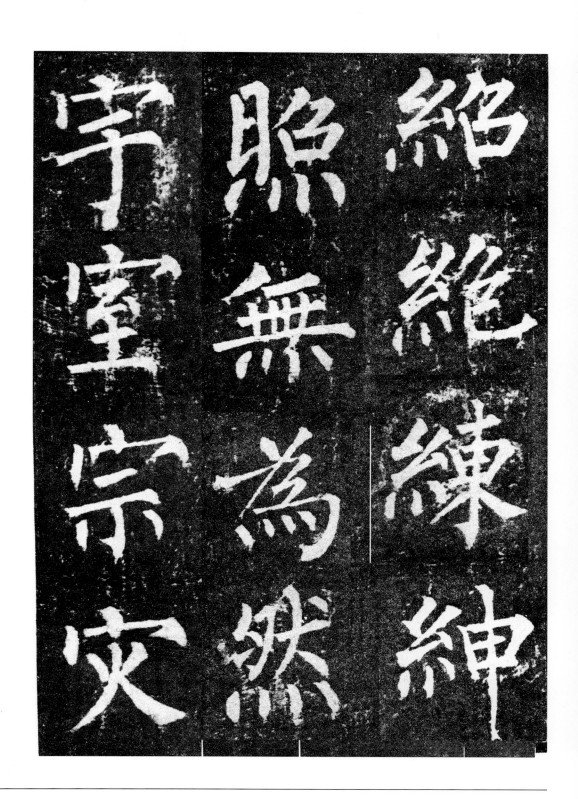

宇寠宗宨　照無為然　絕絁練紳

Chinese Regular Script Calligraphy for Beginners

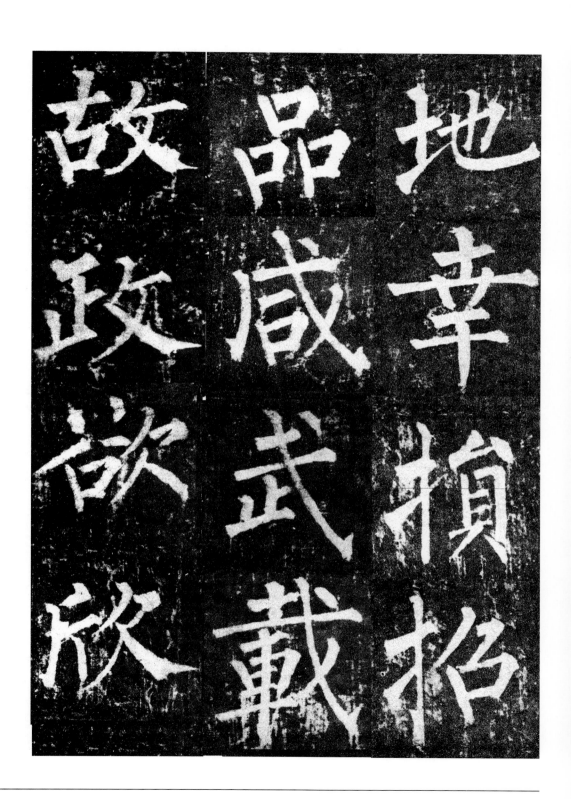

7. *Lotus Sutra* copied
by Xue Chonghui in AD
695 妙法莲花经

常在於其中 經行及坐臥

妙法蓮華經卷第五

大周蓁壟元秊歲次乙未四囗戊寅

朔廿一日戊戌弟子薛崇微奉為

尊長敬造

經行及禪寂　種種寶嚴好　若有信解心　受持讀誦書

若復教人書　及供養經卷　散華香抹香　以須曼瞻蔔

阿提目多伽　勲油常燃之　如是供養者　得無量功德

如虛空無邊　其福亦如是　況復持此經　兼布施持戒

忍辱樂禪定　不瞋不惡口　恭敬於塔廟　謙下諸比丘

遠離自高心　常思惟智慧　有問難不瞋　隨順為解說

若能行是行　功德不可量　若見此法師　成就如是德

應以天華散　天衣覆其身　頭面接足礼　生心如佛想

又應作是念　不久詣道樹　得無漏無為　廣利諸人天

8. Lingfei Canon 灵飞经[靈飛經] attributed to Zhong Shaojing (d. AD 746)

令豪九疑山其女子有郭勺藥趙愛兒王魯
連等並受此法而得道者復數十人或遊玄
州或豪東華方諸臺今見在也南岳魏夫人
也少好道精誠真人因授其六甲趙愛兒者
言此云郭勺藥者漢度遼將軍陽平郭騫女
幽州刺史劉虞別駕漁陽趙該姉也好道得
尸解後又受此符王魯連者魏明帝城門校
尉范陵王伯綑女也亦學道一旦忽委塯李

子期入陸渾山中真人又授此法子期者司

州魏人清河王傳者也其常言此婦狂走云

一旦失所在

上清六甲靈飛隱道脈此真符遊行八方行

此真書當得其人按四極明科傳上清內書

者皆列盟奉脆啟擔乃宣之七百年得付六

人過年限足不得復出洩也其受符皆對齋

瓊宮五帝內思上法

常以正月二月甲乙之日平旦沐浴齋戒入

室東向叩齒九通平坐思東方東極玉真青

帝君諱雲拘字上伯衣服如法乘青雲飛輿

從青要玉女十二人下降齋室之內手執通

靈青精玉符授與地身坐便服符一枚微祝

玉女十真同服黃錦帔紫羅飛羽希頭並積

雲三角髻餘髮散之至臂手執神虎之符乘

九色之鳳白鸞之車飛行上清晏景常陽迴

真下降入地身中地便心念甲戌一旬玉女

諱字如上十真玉女悉降地形仍叩齒六通

洇液六十過畢祝如前太玄之文

上清六甲虛映之道當得至精至真之人乃

得行之旣速致通降而靈氣易發久勤

修之坐在立止長生久視變化萬端行廚卒

致也

九疑真人韓偉遠昔受此方於中岳宋德玄

德玄者周宣王時人服此靈飛六甲得道隱

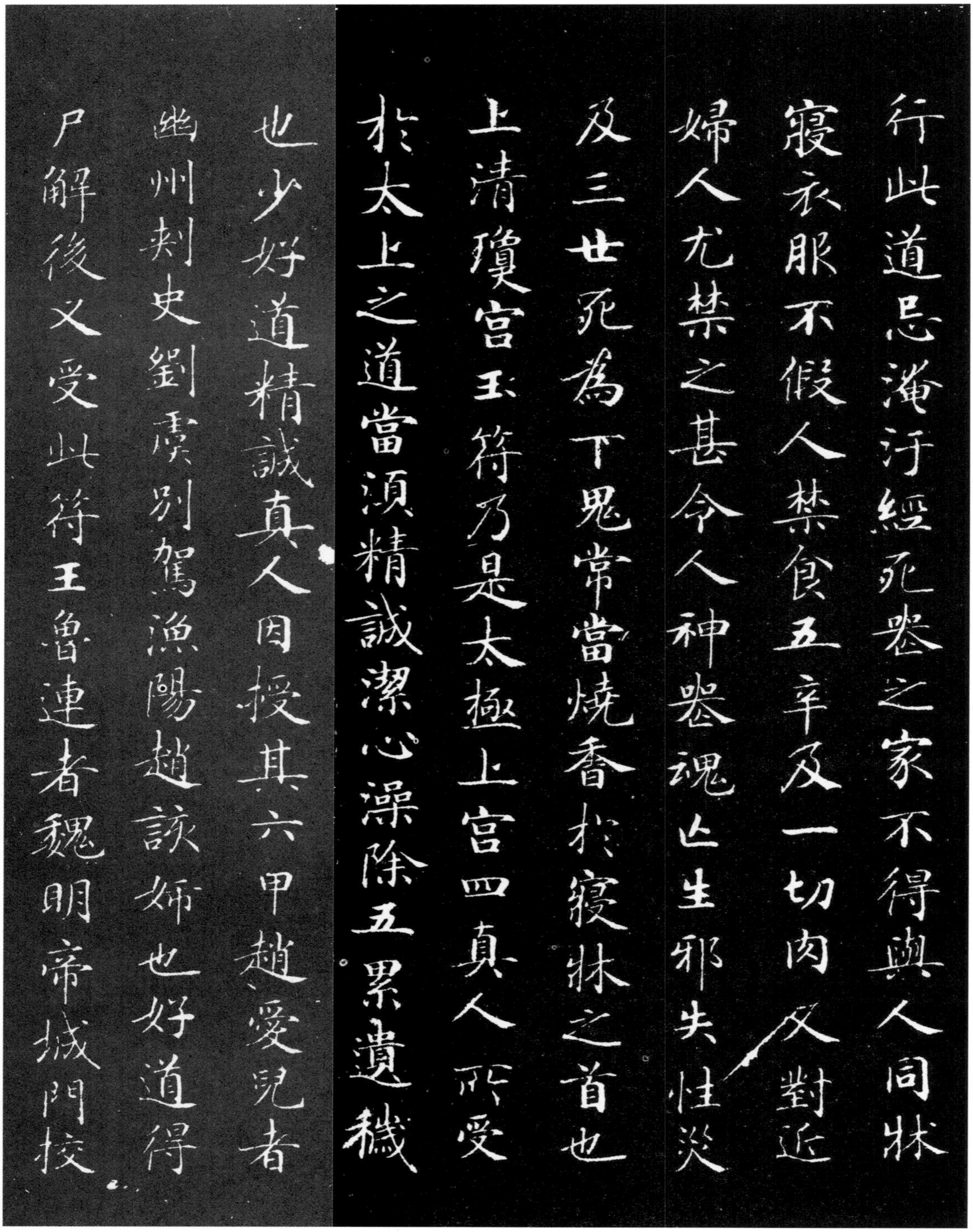

行此道忌淹汙經死喪之家不得與人同牀
寢衣服不假人禁食五辛及一切肉又對近
婦人尤禁之甚令人神喪魂亡生邪失性災
及三世死為下鬼常當燒香於寢牀之首也
上清瓊宮玉符乃是太極上宮四真人所受
於太上之道當須精誠潔心澡除五累遺穢
也少好道精誠真人因授其六甲趙愛兒者
幽州刺史劉虞別駕漁陽趙談姉也好道得
尸解後又受此符王魯連者魏明帝城門校

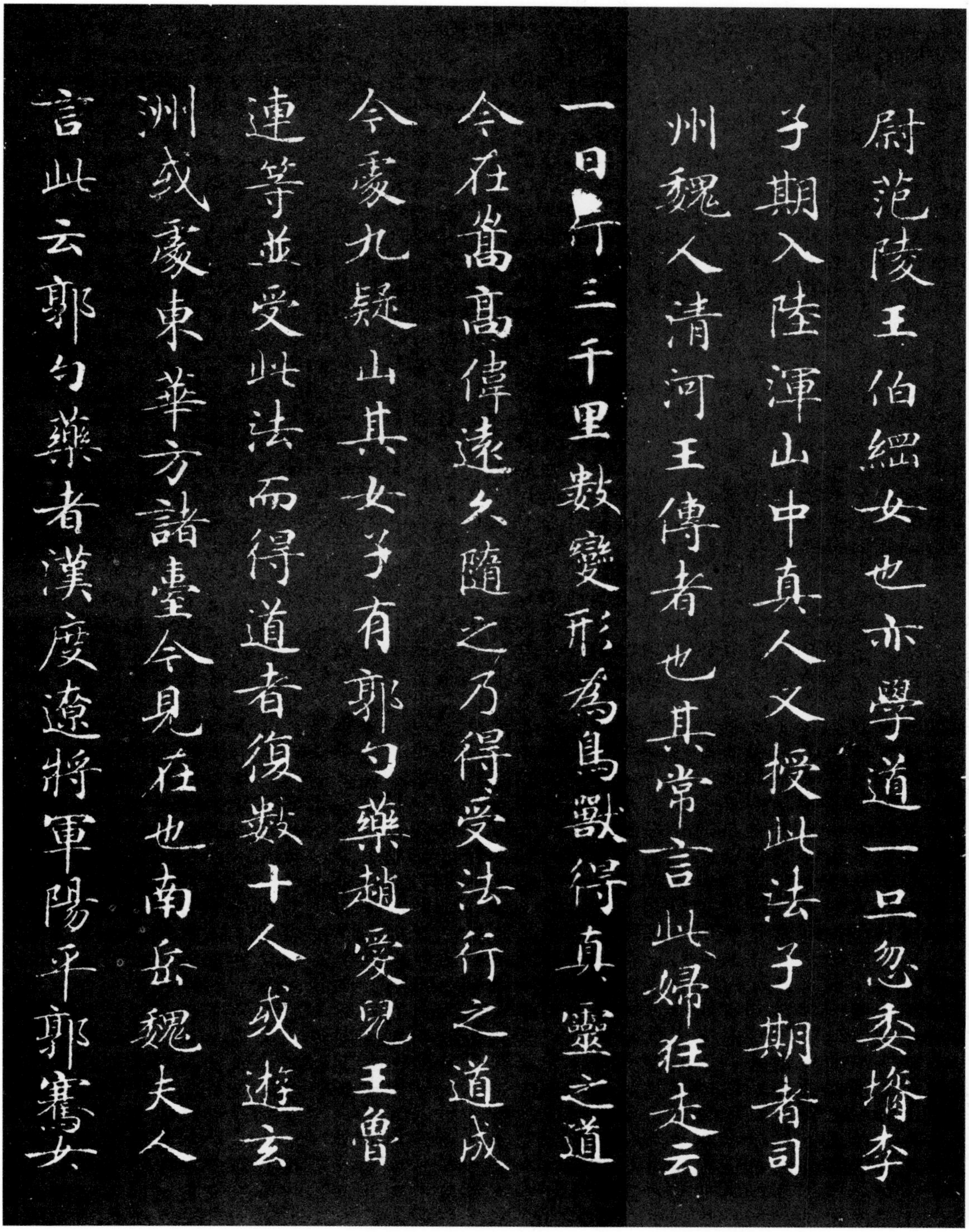

尉范陵王伯綗女也亦學道一旦忽委婚李
子期入陸渾山中真人又授此法子期者司
州魏人清河王傳者也其常言此婦狂走云
一日行三千里數變形為鳥獸得真靈之道
今在嵩高偉遠久隨之乃得受法行之道成
今豪九疑山其女子有郭勺藥趙愛兒王魯
連等並受此法而得道者復數十人或遊玄
洲或豪東華方諸臺今見在也南岳魏夫人
言此云郭勺藥者漢度遼將軍陽平郭騫女

9. "On Pavilion of Drunken Man" written by Su Shi (1031 — 1101)

醉翁亭记

10. "On the Longevity and Springtime Hall" written by Zhao Mengfu (1254 — 1322) 寿[壽]春堂记

興 益
喜 生
幸 作

清 蒲
波 蘭
溪 落

卜 情 有
十 惟 在
居 憬 謂

此 申 昔
老 平 者
流 年 亭

趙之
遶度
過赳

夏又瘕
後名庶
履夌登

姓歌檜
安飲暇
如史繪

11. Du Fu's poems written by Kong Jixun (1792—1842). Kong inherited Ouyang Xun's austere style.

杜甫七律

題張氏隱居二首錄一

春山無伴獨相求伐木丁丁山更幽澗道

餘寒歷○雪石門斜日到林丘不貪夜識

金銀氣遠害朝看麋鹿遊乘興杳然迷出

處對君疑是泛虛舟

贈田九判官

岷使節上青霄河隴降王欵聖朝宛馬

曲江對雨

城上春雲覆苑牆江亭晚色靜年芳林花

著雨燕支溼水荇牽風翠帶長龍武新軍

深駐輦芙蓉別殿謾焚香何時詔此金錢

會暫醉佳人錦瑟旁

奉和賈至舍人早朝大明宮

五夜漏聲催曉箭九重春色醉仙桃旌旗

日暖龍蛇動宮殿風微燕雀高朝罷香烟

攜滿袖詩成珠玉在揮毫欲知世掌絲綸

美池上于今有鳳毛

宣政殿退朝晚出左掖

天門日射黃金榜春殿晴曛赤羽旗宮草

霏霏承委珮鑪烟細細駐遊絲雲近蓬萊

常五色雪殘鳷鵲亦多時侍臣緩步歸青

瑣退食從容出每遲

早朝大明宮呈兩省寮友 賈至

細寫愁仍破萬顆　訝許同憶昨賜露

門下省退朝擘出大明宮金盤玉筯無消

息此日常新任轉蓬

　野望

西山白雪三城戌南浦清江萬里橋海內

風塵諸弟隔天涯涕淚一身遙唯將遲暮

供多病未有涓埃荅聖朝跨馬出郊時極

目不堪人事日蕭條

蜀相

丞相祠堂何處尋錦官城外柏森森映階
碧草自春色隔葉黃鸝空好音三顧頻頻
天下計兩朝開濟老臣心出師未捷身先
死長使英雄淚滿襟

賓至

幽棲地僻經過少老病人扶再拜豈有
文章驚海內漫勞車馬駐江干竟日淹留

發朝夕催人自白頭

送韓十四江東覲省

兵戈不見老萊衣歎息人間萬事非我已

無家尋弟妹君今何處訪庭闈黃牛峽靜

灘聲轉白馬江寒樹影稀此別應須各努

力故鄉猶恐未同歸

野人送朱櫻

西蜀櫻桃也自紅野人相贈滿筠籠數迴

去歲茲辰捧御牀五更三點入鵷行欲知

趨走傷心地正想氤氳滿眼香無路從容

陪語笑有時顛倒著衣裳何人却憶窮愁

日愁日愁隨一綫長

憶昨逍遥供奉班去年今日侍龍顏麒麟

不動鑪烟上孔雀徐開扇影還玉几由來

天北極朱衣只在殿中間孤城此日堪腸

斷愁對寒雲雪滿山

12. Tang-dynasty poems written by Zhang Yuzhao (1828—1894), an important protagonist of the revived "Northern-Wei Stele" style calligraphy

己傳幽花危石

底晚景卧鐘邊

俯仰悲身世溪

雲拂髙

海中月照君池
上樓山雲拂髙
棟天漢入橋流

翁雜陽早春詩

暮聲雜初鴈夜

色酒早秋獨見

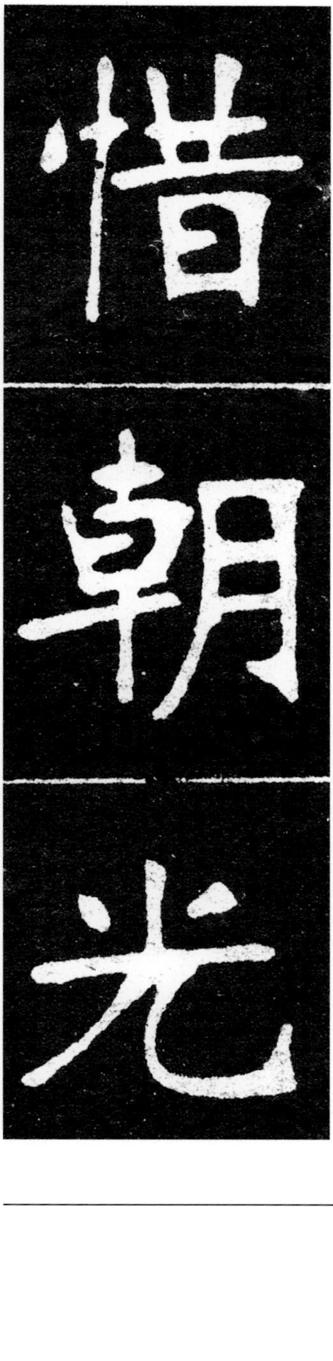
惜朝光

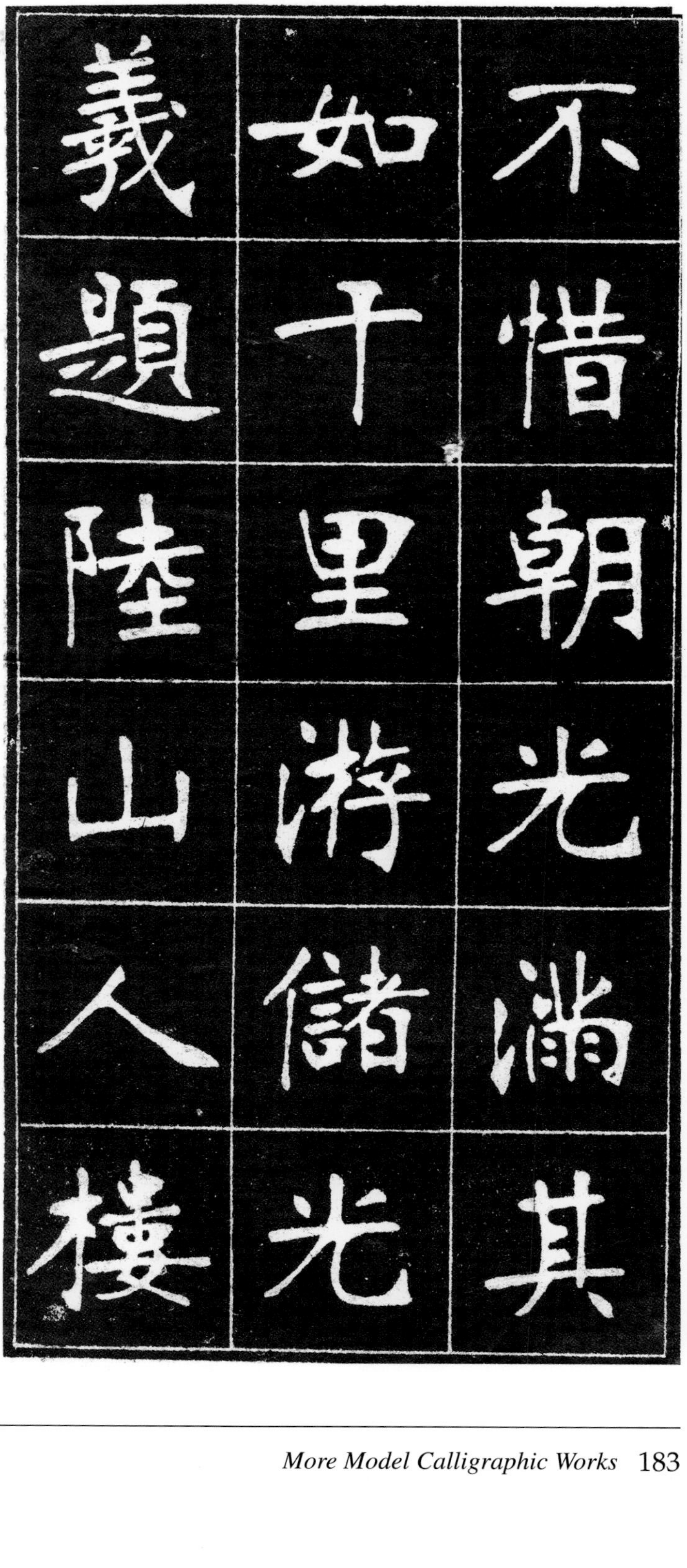
不惜朝光滿其
如千里游儲光
義題陸山人樓

图书在版编目（CIP）数据

怎样写楷书 / 宗建业编著，温晋根编译.
—北京：外文出版社，2007
（怎样做系列）
ISBN 978-7-119-04861-1

I. 怎... II.①宗...②温... III. 楷书–技法（美术）—英文 IV. J292.113.3

中国版本图书馆 CIP 数据核字（2007）第 096751 号

责任编辑　温晋根
封面设计　蔡　荣
插图绘制　宗建业　温晋根　孙树明
策　划　王贤春　李振国　肖晓明　温晋根

外文出版社网址：
http://www.flp.com.cn
外文出版社电子信箱：
info@flp.com.cn
sales@flp.com.cn

怎样写楷书

宗建业　著

*

© 外文出版社
外文出版社出版
（中国北京百万庄大街 24 号
邮政编码 100037）
北京雷杰印刷有限公司印刷
中国国际图书贸易总公司发行
（中国北京车公庄西路 35 号
北京邮政信箱第 399 号　邮政编码 100044）
2007 年（16开）第 1 版第 1 次印刷
2012 年第 1版第 3 次印刷
（英）
ISBN 978-7-119-04861-1
14000（平）
7-E-3761P

AN ILLUSTRATED GUIDE TO
CATS

MARGARET KEENAN

Published in 2009 by TAJ Books International LLP

27, Ferndown Gardens,
Cobham,
Surrey,
UK,
KT11 2BH

www.tajbooks.com

ISBN-13: 978-1-84406-138-6

Printed in China.

AN ILLUSTRATED GUIDE TO
CATS

MARGARET KEENAN

T&J

INTRODUCTION

Our domesticated cat, *FELIS SYLVESTRIS CATUS*, has been part of human society for many thousands of years. Yet it is the least understood of the main domesticated animals, and it retains its mysterious nature and elusive character despite having lived in and around our homes for at least 4,000 years. To many people who give cats homes and affection it is a major part of the cat's attraction—that despite the fact that we feed them, home them, and pour affection on them, they remain a little aloof and always insist on their independence.

Cats became domesticated well after dogs, and also after cattle, sheep, and the other main domesticated animals that have been linked to man. The exact time at which wild cats became domesticated is uncertain, though by 4,000 years ago the first evidence of domesticated cats start to appear in Egyptian paintings. In a wall painting found in Beni Hasan in Egypt, a cat is shown crouching under a chair and clearly part of the domestic life of the family portrayed. But this is not the first indication of the domestication of the cat. A cat's tooth from 9000 B.C. was found in Jericho, Israel, and in the 1980s feline remains from before 5000 B.C were found on the Mediterranean island of Cyprus. As wildcats did not live on Cyprus, this suggests that cats had been taken there, perhaps as a pet.

The mystery of how cats actually became domesticated and became the animal we know today, has inspired many myths and tales. The British author, Rudyard Kipling, as well as giving his tale of how cats became domesticated, also perfectly captures the essential character of cats in his story of "The Cat that Walked by Himself," from the Just So Stories. The tale tells of how cat makes a bargain with woman, who has tamed the other animals like the dog and the horse. The cat is the last of the animals to come into the cave of the Woman, as he is "the cat who walks by himself, and all places are alike to him." Eventually however the cat cannot resist the warm fireplace and warm white milk and shows the woman how useful he can be and makes a bargain with her. He will remain the cat who walks by himself, but in exchange for warm milk and a place by the fireside he will be good to the baby—as long as it does not pull his tail too hard—and kill the mice. Unfortunately he does not make a bargain with the dog or the man, so that in future man throws things at the cat and the dog chases him. Kipling's cat is familiar to us, and also illustrates the complicated relationship that man has had with cats in the west with man's unkindness to cats illustrated by the man's promise that he will always throw something at the cat when he sees him.

The reality is, of course, a bit different! There were two types of small wild cat living around the Egyptian area at the time of their domestication—the African wildcat (Felis silvestris lybica) and the jungle cat (Felis chaus). The generally accepted view is that the more friendly African wildcat took advantage of the developing agrarian communities of the Nile delta as the Egyptians began to grow, and of necessity store, large quantities of grain. As more grain was grown and more was stored against times of shortage, the population of vermin such as rats and mice began to explode. The wildcats would have overcome their initial timidity to hunt this valuable and readily available food source. Maybe the Egyptians began to encourage these welcome vermin controllers, who not only rid them of rats and mice but also hunted the many lethal snakes that lived around the Nile valley. The Egyptians had many domesticated animals already and they readily accepted and appreciated the developing relationship with these small, determined hunters.

The exact time, and the exact process, will never be known for certain. But what is certain it that by 2000 B.C. cats were fully integrated into Egyptian society and that the ancient Egyptians had developed a respect and admiration of cats, so that eventually the cat became a religious symbol, and its image was used on a wide variety of objects.

Cats start appearing in pictures on tomb walls, often sitting under the furniture, or stealing a little morsel from a banquet. The scribe Nebamun liked his cat so much that it was immortalized with him on his tomb wall in Thebes painted in the 18th Dynasty around 1350 B.C., hunting with Nebamun and his family, with the cat holding three birds that it has caught.

Cats eventually became associated with the deity Bastet (or Bast), the goddess of feminine allure, fertility, maternity and the home. Originally Bastet was a local goddess from the town of Bubastis, but when the founder of the twenty-second Dynasty made Bubastis his capital the importance of Bastet increased. Images of Bastet, as an elegant cat or a cat-headed woman, began to be common in Egypt, and though very divine there was something about the homeliness of the cat that made the goddess special for ordinary people. Herodotus, the Greek writer, touring Egypt in the fifth century B.C., noted how popular were both Bastet's temple in Bubastis and her annual festival. He has a lovely description of the importance of cats to the Egyptians describing how when a cat died a natural death, all in the house would shave their eyebrows. The cat would be taken to Bubastis, where it was embalmed and then buried in sacred receptacles. He reported that during spring men and women would sail up the river to Bubastis, singing bawdy songs and celebrating the goddess in a very manner.

The strange finding of thousands of cat mummies at Beni Hassan in the 1800s is a well-known story—as is the fact that eventually the mummies were sold for fertilizer and only a few survived. The reason for the mummies has led to much conjecture—were the cats some form of sacrifice?—several mummified cats had been obviously killed and were only young, under two years of age. Other reports state the fact that it was a capital offence to kill a cat, and any cat that died had to be inspected by a priest to confirm that it had died a natural death.

The idea of cat mummies might seem to us in this age rather strange and a little unsettling, but the statues now held in various museums around the world confirm the Egyptian's knowledge of the cat character and a genuine fondness for this animal that had started out as a uninvited, but useful guest, and had stayed to become an integral part of Egyptian society.

From Egypt, and despite there being a law against the export of cats, cats made their way onto barges on the Nile River, and eventually spread from the Egyptian empire to India, China and Japan—even to Norway, where the Vikings used cats as rat catchers.

The spread of the domestic cat out of Egypt was slow. There is little evidence of the domestic cat in the Greek civilisation, until a cat appears in a marble relief from 500 B.C., in an encounter between a cat and a dog, both on leases and in the presence of two men. No cats have been found in Pompeii, though in later centuries cats had spread throughout the Roman Empire. It is believed that the spread of the cat was eventually assisted by the end of the cult of Bastet—which had survived into the fourth century A.D., but was eventually banned by the Emperor Theodostus I (347–395).

By the 11th century the value of cats as vermin controllers was recognized in France, where they appear in wills and legacies. In Wales their value was recognized in monetary value—the Laws of Hywel Dda from the 10th century gives the amount a cat is worth depending on the age of the cat and its history of vermin control. There were even fines for those who did not care for their cat properly.

However, in the late middle ages in Europe the life of a cat could be difficult. There are records of extreme cruelty being carried out on cats in public, and accusations of witchcraft leveled at those who kept cats. In many European folk tales cats are associated with bad luck and magic; their character was perceived as being one of sly and underhand. This "sneaky" character was reflected in stories, the Brothers Grimm recording one folk tale where the sneaky cat persuades a mouse to set up house with it, and buy a large pot of fat to survive the winter with. The cat regularly sneaks off and steals the fat, and when the winter gets hard and the fat is needed it has all gone. When the mouse finds the pot empty, and scolds the cat, the cat solves the problem by eating up the mouse!

Though there were a few favorable medieval stories or writings of cats it takes a long time in Europe before cats are seen as anything rather than a pest controller and their possibility for being loving pets is recognized. One of the first admirers of cats in modern Europe was Cardinal Richelieu, and cats gradually began to acquire other famous devotees, such as Dr. Samuel Johnson. His friend James Boswell wrote how Dr. Johnson would go out and buy meat for his cat (named Hodge) rather than asking his servant to do it, so that the servant would not resent his cat and take a dislike to it.

Cats in other parts of the world seem to have fared rather better than in Europe. The prophet Mohammed forbade all cruelty to animals, but was particularly fond of cats. There is a story that one day Muhammad's cat was sleeping on his cloak when he was called to prayers, he took off his cloak rather than disturb his cat.

As domestic cats moved out of Egypt they moved through Persia and India to the Far East. They were not favored in the Zoroastrian tradition, though their importance was recognized, and even with the advent of Islam hostility to cats remained in this part of the world. This suspicion of cats extended into India, where they were well known by 500 A.D.—even now cats are rarely kept as pets there. Cats arrived in China early in the Common Era, and were well known by the Tang Dynasty. It is the artists of this dynasty that first began to paint and draw cats in an affectionate and realistic manner—much more so than can be found in the European tradition. Around about the seventh century cats were introduced into Japan, where they became highly favored pets of the Emperor and his court. At first rare, cats soon began to multiply, but they continued to be treated well and were highly valued throughout the Far East for their ability to kill rats.

INTRODUCTION

Cats were brought to America by the first European settlers in the seventeenth century. Even now it is possible to distinguish genetically between the cats whose ancestors came from those brought in by the English around New England, and those cats descended from Dutch stock in New York. As in Europe, cats were not immediately popular in America. The famous witch trials of Salem illustrate how cats were seen in the seventeenth century, with accusations of "shape-changing" into cat-like figures being levelled at some of the women accused of witchcraft.

Gradually cats began to gain status in America and Europe, and though cats had been bred in an organized fashion in Thailand for centuries, the idea began to gain popularity in the west. The first official cat show in America was held in Madison Square Gardens, New York in 1895, and the American Cat Fanciers' Association was founded in 1906. The organizers of these organizations were not just focused on breeding "pedigree" cats, a core purpose for setting up these organizations was to bring better treatment for all cats and to raise both the cat's status and their well-being.

Cats now rival dogs as the most popular pet in North America and Europe, though there is still, unfortunately, much ill-treatment of cats, both deliberate and through ignorance. The role of organizations like the CFA in bringing better treatment for cats is still important today.

In the last 100 years the change in the status of cats has been reflected in popular art and literature. T.S. Eliot's Book of Practical Cats, is a charming series of poems written about strange and wonderful cats, including Macavity the Mystery Cat and Bustopher Jones—the Cat About Town. In 1981 the book was turned into the hit musical Cats—an unlikely transposition of verse to music!

Nowadays we are used to seeing cats in cartoon strips, as characters in animated films and as illustrations on cards and posters. There are many modern artists who take inspiration from their cats, and though 100 years ago cats may have been seen in paintings as accessories or symbols—often in connection with woman's sexuality—nowadays they are also drawn for their own individual nature. The Scottish artist, Elizabeth Blackadder, is a noted painter of flowers and cats. These are not pedigree cats, but they are special because they are painted with a true affection and understanding of their nature.

It has taken several thousand years, but the role of cats as respected and loved parts of the household is once again popular and accepted.

What is a cat?

The domesticated cat, is a member of the large cat family, the Felidae, part of the order of Carnivora. The Felidae are the most specialized members of the Carnivora, the only ones who eat only meat, with strong well-developed canine and carnissal teeth and a digestive tract suitable for the digestion of meat. The premolar and the first molars, which together compose the carnassial pair on each side of the mouth, function to shear meat like a pair of scissors. Cat's tongues have sharp spines, or papillae, which are used for retaining and ripping flesh from a carcass. The papillae are small backward-facing hooks that contain keratin and assist in a cat's grooming. The ears of a cat can move independently of each other, a cat can move its body in one direction and point its ears in another.

The cat family is a successful and adaptable group of animals, found all over the world except the Australasian and Antarctica continents. They have flexible, muscular bodies, acute senses and lightening reflexes. Their flexible spines mean they can turn and twist, and by using their spines in a certain way cats can reach high speeds—though as this uses a high amount of their body's energy, cats cannot retain these high speeds for any length of time and therefore tend not to be known for their speed endurance.

Most members of the cat family are solitary, that is, they prefer to hunt and live alone. There are exceptions, such as lions, that live in matriarchal groups. All cats have certain traits in common. They are adapted for prowling and hunting with large eyes and flexible pupils that can see in near darkness—though cats cannot see any better than any other animal in pitch darkness! They also have acute hearing and smell and outer hairs that are sensitive to the slightest pressure.

The small wildcat is thought to have spread out from its Ice Age beginnings in Europe some 250,000 years ago to Asia and Africa. They are found in the jungles of Africa to the cold conifer forests of Scotland, from the deserts of the Sahara to the rain forests of Asia.

The anatomy of the domestic cat has changed little from its wildcat ancestor; its brain is about one quarter smaller than that of the ancestral African wildcat, as it is not so dependent on its wits for survival. The intestines are shorter and the hormone producing glands in the body are smaller. Domestic cats are also noisier than their wildcat relatives. These differences reflect the environment that domestic cats inhabit—safer and easier than their wild cousins.

Cats are digitigrades, they walk on their toes and the bones of the feet form the main part of the lower part of the visible leg. Like all felines cats walk placing their hind paws almost directly in the print of the forepaws, minimizing noise and visible tracks. Unlike dogs and most mammals, cats walk by moving both legs on one side and then both legs on the other. By having retractable claws cats can keep them sharp by preventing wear and tear on hard surfaces and silently stalk their prey.

Cats have compound hair follicles with up to six primary hairs from each follicle, each surrounded by finer secondary hairs. Northern breeds have dense coats with insulating down that provides efficient insulation, and when cold the hair erects trapping a layer of air that will keep a cat warm. Cats living in hot climates shed their coat of down hair and blood vessels in the skin dilate helping to speed the loss of body heat. Cats do not sweat, but will lick their fur to lose heat as the evaporating saliva carries away the body heat.

Cats are well equipped against the extremes of heat and cold, but they have a tendency to heat prostration and frostbite. If a cat's fur becomes wet it loses its insulating properties and cats are therefore at risk of hypothermia if they become wet and cold.

Cats have two types of hair specialized for sensation. The whiskers (vibrissae) are thick, stiff hairs found on the head, throat and forelegs. Tylotrichs are large single hairs found all over the skin and act like short whiskers. The whiskers are highly mobile and sensitive; they are developed when kittens are in the womb. The whiskers can be moved backward or forward, and the whiskers around the eyes and cheeks help a cat to avoid dangers as it explores its environment.

The skeleton of a domestic cat shows its ancestry; it is light and supple and made for speed and agility. The slender, but robust legs support a narrow ribcage and the highly supple spine. The flexible spine and pliant muscles enable a cat to curl up or rotate its body by 180 degrees in midair. The cat's shoulder is very different to ours—it is an amazing collection of muscle, and the forelimb of a cat is attached to the rest of the body by only muscle. This allows for freedom of movement in the shoulder, which lengthens a cat's stride and increases its range of motion.

It is generally accepted that cats are "color blind," as tests have shown that the color sensitive cone cells on a cat's retina are sensitive to blue and green, but not red. In normal life color appears meaningless to cats. Cat's eyes are more sensitive than ours however, with more motion-detecting rods, which also assists them in seeing in low-light conditions. Cats cannot resolve detail sharply as the lens in the eye is large in order for them to gather as much light as possible in low-light conditions. The most spectacular adoption of a cat's eye is the tapetum lucidum, the layer of reflective cells behind the retina. These mirrorlike cells bounce light back through the retina to give a heightened ability to interpret information. The protruding eyes of cats give a wider angle of vision than ours and they also have superior peripheral vision.

The cat's eyes are perfectly adapted to assist the cat in being an opportunistic hunter, especially effective during low light hours such as dawn and dusk—the time when our domestic cats are most active.

Our domestic cats have excellent hearing, perfect for listening for the smallest rustle of a small rodent. A cat can hear much higher frequencies than we can, though, like us, they do lose this higher range as they become older. Their sense of smell, while not as acute as a dog, is still much better than ours. They have twice as many smell-sensitive cells in their noses than humans, and taste buds specialized to detect the amino acids of meat. Cats can taste sour, bitter and salty tastes, but are unable to detect sweet tastes.

Domestic Cat Behavior

Of all domesticated animals, cats have changed the least in both their genetics and their behavior. We consider it amazing if our cats learn any tricks, and generally aim for them to be reasonably well-behaved and affectionate. The main difference between the domestic cat and its wildcat cousins is sociability and the ability to be affectionate to humans. Although recent breeding efforts have attempted to exaggerate this trait, all domestic cats do inherently posses this ability. Some authorities claim that the effectiveness of breeding for sociability is unproven: indeed, there will never be genetic changes as a result of domestication or selective breeding—rather the breeding influences which regulatory genes are working—those genes which switch other genes on or off.

What elements of a cat's behavior can we influence, and what elements are immutable? And how does this, or should this, direct the way we respond and relate to our cats?

One of the behaviors of cat that we cannot change is the amount they sleep! Cats sleep an incredible amount—up to sixteen hours a day, though thirteen to fourteen is more normal. How much a cat sleeps will vary: some cats are just plain lazier than others, some breeds are less active, and as a cat gets older its sleeping habits will change, and it will sleep more—but not necessarily at night. Why cats sleep so much is not yet understood, though in kittens growth hormones are only released during sleep. Cats need sleep to maintain good health and body functions.

Domestic cats do tend to have their lively periods at dawn and dusk, which can cause problems for their human owners, though once a cat's activity pattern is known, a sensible owner can use this knowledge to work to their, and the cat's, mutual benefit.

Domestic cats are not necessarily "solitary" animals as such, they can be quite social, but unlike dogs, they do not have a pack mentality, and they take care of their own needs and do not hunt in groups. Domestic cats can be quite happy in large social groups, and feral groups of cats are well known. If domestic cats are brought up together they can be very social and indeed some cats will pine if they are used to a large social group and become solitary. However, there are some domestic cats who are never happy in groups and much prefer to be a single cat in a household—it all depends on the character of the cat.

After millennia of domestication cats have come to look on their human companions as their main source of food and shelter. It is generally considered that cats have been selectively bred to keep the kitten in them, and though more than other domesticated animals cats can survive without humans, if a cat is in contact with humans from an early age it ultimately looks to us as a life-long parent. We have a responsibility to our cats to provide them with companionship and affection, though some cats will need proactive attention less than others, all domestic cats need us socially in some way. One of the many characteristics that some owners can find hard to accept is a cat's desire to hunt. We have to accept that most cats will hunt, and though in some breeds this tendency has been reduced, for the majority of those of us who have cats, the cat's need to hunt has to be managed. Indeed, for many people the cats main function is still to keep vermin down, but for those cat owners who live in an urban or semiurban environment and wish to keep some wildlife in their garden, knowing how and why cats hunt can be useful in managing that trait if necessary.

Domestic cats do not hunt from hunger and even the fattest and best-fed cat will still stalk birds and mice if they are around. Hunting is a core element of the cat's character: they hunt because they want to, because it is hard-wired in their brains. Cats will use the same techniques that their big brothers do—the same techniques that we have all seen on wildlife program. They will use long grass to stalk birds. Crouching low, they will slowly move through the grass or your flower patch employing every inch of cover that they can. They learn where mice and small mammals have their runs, and will potentially wait until one moves along one of these corridors.

It is no use shouting at a cat if they bring a "present" to you of a dead bird or shrew. It is thought that they are showing you that they can be a useful member of their cat "group," or that like young animals they are showing their parents that they are capable of hunting. If you wish to have birds in your garden, then you can cut down on the death-rate by putting a bell on your cat's collar, or follow the lead of many Australian states, whose local laws compel cat owners to keep their cats in around sunset and sunrise and keep your cat indoors at these vulnerable times for birds.

The sociability of cats is very variable. Though cats always hunt alone, their ability to mix with other cats and domestic pets does vary. Cat sociability is matriarchal—in feral communities it is a group of closely related females who form the colony. Male kittens are gradually ejected by the females to form loose groups of male cats, who will tolerate each other if there is plenty of food around, but fight if food is short or there are breeding females in season.

In the domestic setting the sex of your cat, and whether it is neutered or not, will have a major effect on its character. When there are a number of cats in a household, the top cat will often change, but if the group includes breeding females these are often at the top of the pile, with neutered males and females being lower in status. An ill or injured cat will lose some of its status, and if this happens it is a good sign to a cat owner that one of their cats might be in need of medical care.

Cats like to mark their territory, and will do this to by either scratching on a highly visible marker or by leaving a powerful scent marker. Both male and female cats will mark their territories, and even when they are neutered many cats continue to leave scent markers. Cats which spray in their home are often under some form of stress, and owners will need to look at their environment to see if any changes have happened—such as a new neighbourhood cat, or changes in their own pattern of behavior, such as being away from the house more often.Cats also like to communicate by touch, which they use both with each other and in their contact with humans. Cats enjoy being stroked, but nearly all cats have some limit over which the stroking becomes excessive and they display aggressive behavior—though it will always apologise afterwards and request more attention!

It is useful to be able to understand your cat's communications—though of course, we will never be able to speak proper cat! Cat sounds are divided into three sorts: murmurs, which include purring and the soft-sounding chirp used for greeting and registering pleasure; vowel sounds which include the classic miaow and can mean ' hello', 'I'm here', 'where is my food', and 'where are you?' amongst others; high intensity sounds which are usually used when other cats are around and occasionally move into the sounds of a cat in pain or distress.

A cat's body language is also an important part of how it communicates, and you will soon learn the most vital signs; ears back mean 'go away' or 'I'm scared and will attack'; a relaxed cat looks gentle and will in likelihood be purring—or asleep. Don't forget, always be gentle with your cat and do not make sudden movements around it—you could startle it and cause them to suddenly turn on you. A cat's behavior is as much about how the humans around it act as about the cat itself.

Cats can be trained to a certain basic level, it is certainly possible to train a cat to have appropriate behavior in your home to an extent. There are techniques such as using a water spray when a cat is about to do something it shouldn't—like clawing the furniture or curtains. Cats will learn to respond to a soft tap on the nose and a sharp "no," and eventually will learn to respond to just the word "no." There are many books available on cat behavior and how to modify a cat's behavior if it is causing you serious problems. However all cat owners must accept certain patterns of cat behavior as mentioned above—or else your cat would not be a cat. Also, like all animals, as they age, cats can sometimes become forgetful, or distressed and an elderly cat might well need more regular assurance and attention to keep it happy.

Behavioral problems can be avoided by sensible behavior of the owner. If a cat claws your favorite piece of furniture, then you can use the water spray technique—but it might be easier to ensure that you do not let the cat into a room where your good furniture is unless it has human company, and make sure it is well provided with scratching posts. A good solid, readily accessible scratching post will assist in avoiding damaged furniture.

Stalking your ankles can be both painful for you and the cat if you trip over it. Again it can be remedied by the judicial use of a water pistol, or by ensuring that your cats have enough toys to play with and is not getting bored enough to find your ankles so attractive. Play is extremely important to both kittens and cats—even quite elderly cats can show a younger side if you find a toy that they can enjoy. They might not play with it as long as a younger cat, but play for all ages of cats is important to help them develop, and maintain, a happy disposition. This is particularly important if, for some reason, you have to have an indoor cat. Cats who are allowed outside on a regular basis will be able to find many things to distract them, but an indoor cat can become depressed and lazy, unless you provide it with play opportunities and toys. Scratching posts, bouncing ping-pong balls, lots of empty boxes to hide in, or a professional cat activity center will all help alleviate boredom. Be careful and keep plastic bags and bits of wool or small buttons out of the way—anything that could asphyxiate or choke a cat.

Jumping on surfaces can be a problem—cats enjoy being high up so that a kitchen surface or dining table is ideal. Practical ways of dealing with this include to block off tempting locations and apply lots of double sided sticking tape to surfaces until the cat learns avoid that spot. Always put food away so that a cat is not tempted to steal—there are some behaviors that are inherent in a cat and is not fair to expect a cat to not investigate the tasty smell of a piece of cooked chicken.

Many cats enjoy the taste of your favorite houseplant, and it can be disconcerting to find odd lumps taken out of a favored plant. This is a problem not only because of the damage to the plant, but because many plants are poisonous to cats. To prevent cats eating plants is never going to be easy—though there are sprays that can be used to make a plant taste bitter. It is also advisable to ensure that cats have easy access to some form of greenery—a grass box is an ideal solution if you do not have a garden with grass in it or you keep your grass very short. Cats like to be able to chew on long leaves—the average suburban lawn is not what they are looking for. If you have a cat that is a big plant eater, then it is probably wise to check whether any of the plants you have are poisonous and remove them from the vicinity of the cat—lilies in gardens can be a particular problem.

INTRODUCTION

Choosing your cat

Whether you choose a pedigree cat or a "moggy," there will be things you will need to do to your house and garden and questions you will need to ask yourself which will help you choose the cat for you.

Do you want a house cat? Maybe you do not want a kitten that might get under your feet, maybe an older cat would you suit you better? Do you still want to attract birds into your garden? Do you want a single cat or maybe two or more? Do you already have other pets that the cat will need to socialise with? Do you have children and how old are they? Are they used to pets?

Do you go out to work? Or maybe you stay at home and would like to have a lap cat, rather than a cat that prefers to be out in the garden? Which sex cat would you prefer? The answers to these questions will help you decide what sort of cat will best suit your circumstances and ensure that you choose a cat that will be comfortable with your lifestyle and home.

If you decide that you would like a pedigree cat, then many of the breeds have clear character traits. Read the breed profile, though while appearance of pedigree cats will be consistent, personality traits will vary. The Oriental cats, the Siamese, Burmese and the Abyssinians, tend to be attention demanding, they are gregarious and often vocal and demand the most activity—whereas Longhairs require the least. For cats that are affectionate Longhairs tend to be the most giving, and are also a lot less destructive than the Orientals and the Siamese. If you have other cats then introducing a Siamese or Burmese cat into the household might be difficult as these are the least friendly.

Do your research, then when you have decided what breed would suit your needs, find a breeder of that type of cat who has a good reputation—ask your local vet or check with the breed society for recommended breeders. Many breeds now have breed societies, which ensure that the breed is being bred properly, and that set standards of care and quality. Visit a number of breeders in person, compare their facilities and prices—buying a good quality pedigree cat, especially if you wish to show it, will not be cheap—and if you can, take someone along with you who knows about the breed and can advise you.

Both parents of any kittens you choose must be registered with the relevant breed registry, and discuss with the breeder about any hereditary diseases that may be prevalent in the breed you are choosing. You will have a much better socialised kitten if it is from a breeder who raises their cats in the home and has been handling the kittens from a young age, rather than one who keeps the mothers in a separate unit. You should always be able to see the mother, and if possible the father—though many breeders do not keep the tom to which their queen has been mated—nevertheless check on the history of the father and whether there are any problems with health or behavior.

Breeders should ensure that kittens have been seen by a vet and vaccinated before they are sold. They should not be ready to go before they are under eight weeks old. A kitten around ten to twelve weeks old is about the right time for it to leave for a new home—by this time the mother will usually be getting rather tired of her kittens and they will be quite independent!

Non-pedigree cats are now the world's favorite family pet. Random breeding means that non-pedigree cats do not have a definitive appearance or temperament, though in general they will be independent but affectionate, they will be robust and playful and they will have that hybrid vigor that is nature's way of selecting the fittest and strongest animals. The choice of colors and patterns will be wide, and of course, the type of coat is variable from smooth and soft to long and hairy.

If you decide that the ordinary "moggy," or non-pedigree cat will suit you fine, then there are number of options for you to find the one for you. Be careful with the 'cats for sale' section of your local newspaper, as the history of cats for sale this way maybe uncertain. The best option is to find a cat through friends and contacts, or to contact your local veterinary clinic, that may well have a notice board with cats needing homes. If you choose a cat through these options do make sure that the kittens have been examined by a vet first and treated for internal parasites such as roundworms, and external parasites such as ear mites.

Cat rescue shelters always have plenty of gorgeous cats needing new homes. A good shelter will assist you in choosing the cat or kitten for you, and will advise you on how to look after it and what its temperament is like. They will answer the questions you will need to ask, such as why it was handed in, what is its known medical history and has the rescue center done any behavior testing. Many cats end up in a rescue shelter through no fault of their own, and make wonderful and loving pets. Cat rescue shelters are the ideal place if you wish to look for an older cat, as well as for a kitten.

The first days at home

When you arrive home with your new cat or kitten, keep them confined to an area with the doors and windows closed. Have a litter tray ready in a private corner before you let them out of the carrier. Place their bed and feeding bowl in a quiet place away from draughts and be very quiet and calm.

A new kitten must be allowed to inspect its new home. Don't leave them on their own: offer them a little food and keep an eye on it until it goes to sleep. It might be tempting to let the family or children play with him, but be very gentle at first. They will have just left their family behind and will be distressed and a little frightened. They will need lots of gentle care and cuddles until their confidence has built up

If you have had cats previously your home and garden will probably be "cat proofed," though it is probably a good idea to give it a quick check. You will need to keep your new cat or kitten inside for the first couple of weeks to make sure it acclimatizes to its new environment and feels safe. If you have a garden and want the cat to be able to access it freely then the best option is to install a cat flap—if you live in an area with many cats you may need to install one that is activated by a magnet on your cat's collar.

Make sure there is somewhere your new cat and kitten can sleep and feel safe. Many cats will choose their own sleeping places, but you can encourage them to certain spots by providing a cat bed, or a soft towel on a chair. Always make sure that these are washable—they will need to be regularly washed to provide your cat with a hygienic sleeping place. Cats will need their own cat bowls and utensils. Some cats do not like the smell of plastic bowls, so will need to be provided with ceramic bowls. These will be available at a pet shop. They will need to be washed daily to keep your cat free of stomach problems.

To transport your cat around, to the vet for instance or if you need to take it to a cattery while you are away, buy a good quality cat carrier. A cardboard box carrier may be suitable for one or two journeys, but they do not last and can be clawed out of by a nervous cat. Let your cat become accustomed to its carrier—do not put away, but leave it around the house where the cat can use it and feel safe in it. Then when it is used for a journey, they will feel more at ease and safe than in a carrier they are only put in for bad things!

Introduce your cat to your garden; walk around the garden with the cat. The first time your cat goes outside make sure it is hungry, you will then be able to tempt the cat back to you with food. It is possible to make your garden more cat friendly and persuade it to stay there rather than haunt your neighbour's garden by ensuring that there are plenty of places for it to snooze. Smooth wood, stone or brick surfaces absorb the heat and provide the perfect environment for a cat wishing to soak up the warmth. Shrubs provide the shade a cat needs when the sun is high. A toilet area will help you to dispose of your cat's waste more easily and can be provided by an area of well-dug fine soil in a sheltered part of the garden. Some cats prefer bark as a toilet area as this does not make their paws muddy.

Cats need grass, it is a natural medicine for relieving bile and sourness and is particularly useful for cats that are prone to hairballs. The creation of a play area in your garden will not only entertain the cat, but also protect the more delicate areas of the garden from his attentions. A scratching post is good way of helping a cat to keep in shape, and prevent your furnishing being used as an alternative! Avoid having a fishpond in your garden—for obvious reasons, but a clean supply of drinking water is welcomed. You might wish to install a decorative pebble pool where cats can drink without falling in. Provide an escape route for your cat, in case a stray dog or cat gets in—a high wall, or mature tree will give it a safe place in these circumstances, as well as providing that all important look out that all cats seem to feel essential.

If you are a keen gardener then you may have to reconsider how you manage your garden. Pesticides and chemicals must only be used with extreme caution, any cat that accidentally gets something on his coat and licks it off could fall dangerously ill. Slug pellets are another source of danger, not only to cats of course, and it advisable to use only environmentally friendly pellets or try other methods of slug control. This may be the time to try organic gardening avoiding the use of chemicals in your garden!

Cats look for the easy life, so if you provide it with the perfect garden it is a lot less likely to stray into other gardens.

If you do not want your cat to wander too much, then it may be appropriate to have your garden fenced. Most cats will take a fence as a subconscious boundary to their territory. If a hedge is planted next to a fence this will make it extra harder for a cat to climb over. But cats being what they are, they will surely climb over it eventually, so make sure there is an easy access route back in, so that the cat does not injure itself jumping down from a high fence. Perhaps a tree by the side of the fence—this will also provide a cat with the perfect place to look down on its surroundings!

There are certain plants that are highly toxic to cats, and it might be advisable to remove them from your garden—especially if you find that your cat is a plant nibbler. It is advisable to avoid growing lily of the valley, laburnum and foxgloves. Most of all it is advisable not to grow members of the Lily family, these are highly toxic to cats and even the pollen which can get brushed onto a cat's coat and then groomed off can cause problems. Less than one leaf eaten by a cat can cause kidney failure.

Cats and traffic do not go well together, and though some cats appear to develop road sense, most seem to employ the method of running across the road as quickly as possible in the apparent hope that no cars will be coming. Though you can never completely remove the danger of a road to cats, try and encourage your cat to stay in your garden by giving it everything it needs there. If you live by a very busy road, then it is perhaps advisable not to have a cat as a pet, and perhaps look at another option for a companion.

Feeding your cat the right sort of food is vital if your cat is to live a long and healthy life. All cats need meat in their diet—cats will not survive on a meat-free diet as due to their genetics they must have certain types of amino acids and taurine. These are essential to the function of a cat's eyes and heart, and can only be found in meat. You cannot have a vegetarian cat.

Young kittens will be weaned by the time that you get them from a breeder, but when you first have a kitten you will need to feed it small amounts four times a day. Use a good proprietary food and ensure that if you are feeding a dry food that you provide plenty of water. This is true for a cat of any age—and don't forget—cats should not be given cow's milk as they find it difficult to digest. If you want to give your cat milk, use one of the specially formulated cat's milk, which are available from most supermarkets and pet shops.

As your cat gets older it will need food that gives it the right sort of minerals and vitamins to enable it to be active and grow. You can treat it occasionally to a little cheese, boiled chicken or fish, and give it some oily fish once a week to eliminate fur balls. Do not let your cat become fussy, which they can, and move to feeding them twice a day. When your cat is fully grown do not allow it to put on too much weight as it will put a strain on his heart and other functions. Make sure you give your cat the recommended amount and occasionally change the food—cats, like humans, get bored of having the same food all the time.

As your cat becomes elderly, its needs change along with its behavior. It will sleep more and will need a diet that has similar levels of fat and protein, with a high digestibility. Any major changes in your cat's eating diets could mean a sign of a more serious illness and it should be taken to the vet immediately.

If you are in any doubts about what to feed your cat, always ask your vet's advice, and remember, always ensure that your cat has plenty of fresh water to drink.

Grooming

A healthy cat will groom itself; in fact, a cat can spend thirty percent of its waking time in grooming. But all cats need a helping hand and it is important that you learn to groom your cat so that it is happy while you do it. The best way is to start when the cat is young and it can then become accustomed to the feel of a brush or a comb. If you get a cat when it is older and it appears not to be used to grooming, start slowly and do a little at any one time. Reward the cat with some favorite titbits, and eventually it will come to enjoy the experience. Grooming a cat can become a very important part of your relationship with it, and it should be enjoyable for both of you. There are many types of combs and brushes on the market, talk to someone experienced with cats to find the best sort of tool for your cat. Grooming a cat is also important because you can check your cats for fleas and mites at the same time, as well as give your cat a general health check.

To neuter or not to neuter?

Unless you are intending to breed from your cat, it is advisable to have it neutered. The operation for male cats is simple and quick, the operation for females is more complicated and they will need time to recover. However, recent advances in cat surgery mean that neutering a female cat is much less a major operation than previously. You will find that a neutered cat makes a much easier companion. Neutered cats live longer, and though some cats gain weight, with an appropriate diet this is not a problem. A male cat should be neutered any age—

preferably the sooner the better so that it does not start wandering or be at risk of catching infectious diseases such as FIV and FeLV from other cats. Female cats should be neutered before their first season. It is not advisable to let a female cat have "just one litter."

Pedigree Cats

Cats have been around for millennia, but in Europe and America it is only in the last hundred years that the "breeding" of a cat has become important. The first cat shows were held in the late 1800s—and since then the breeding of cats has become highly popular—though it should be stated here that by far the majority of cats in America and Europe are still non-pedigrees!

Within the last fifty years there has been an explosion of new cat breeds. All of these new breeds are a result of careful breeding, but some come from breeding on from a chance mutation, such as the Scottish Fold Ear, are some are the result of selective breeding for certain traits, such as the development of the Birman.

Cat breeds are divided into two types: the first are those that appeared naturally in free-breeding populations. Many of these are characterized by coat color or pattern and genetically these are usually "recessives" that breed true. Other breeds, like the Manx, are a result of distinctive mutations. Some breeds developed naturally into types that were later recognized as breeds—such as the Norwegian Forest Cat,

The second type are those breeds which have been bred more recently, and where there has been a direct decision by a breeder about which characteristics they wish to see in the progeny of the cats from which they are breeding. More new breeds appeared in the world from this way of breeding cats than in the whole of the history of domestic cats preceding it. Though some of this breeding has exaggerated some positive characteristics there have been occasions where not so positive effects have been breed into a breed.

The breeding of pedigree cats is regulated by various registries, the largest being the Cat's Fancier's Association (CFA) founded in 1906. It tends to have a purist philosophy, whereas the most liberal of the registries is the International Cat Association (TICA) founded in 1979. This registry accepts new breeds more rapidly than other registries, and thus encourages new breeds and experimentation. Britain's Governing Council of the Cat Fancy (GCCF) was formed in 1910 and falls somewhere between the other two. Most European countries have several registries, but at least one from each country belongs to the Federation Internationale Feline (FiFe) founded in 1949. FIFe's policy is similar to the GCCF: both organizations frown upon breeding for types associated with known defects, such as white-haired, blue-eyed cats, which have a predilection for deafness.

The original coat of the wild cat was of color-banded or "agouti" hair, with the first mutation to a single non-agouti color happening when the cats no longer needed camouflage. It is likely that this first mutation was for black hair with other mutations for red, white and dilutions of solid colors coming along later—and all contributing to the color range available today.

Traditionally western cat colors are black, its dilute blue, red and its dilute cream, and their bicolor versions, and white. The traditional eastern colors are chocolate and its dilute lilac, and cinnamon and its dilute fawn. Many colors have now been transposed from one group to the other so British shorthairs are now accepted in lilac and other eastern colors, while Burmese are accepted in red and cream.

ABYSSINIAN

The Abyssinian is a natural breed of domesticated cat believed to originate from one Egyptian female kitten called Zula that was taken from a port in Alexandria, Egypt, by a British soldier and brought to England. The breed was developed when Zula was bred with an English tabby, and the most 'Abyssinian' looking kitten of her litter bred with its mother to splice the Abby gene. It is believed all Abyssinians in Europe, the Americas, and Australia are descended from Zula, but there has been at least one and possibly as many as three Abyssinians introduced from Libya (or less likely Egypt) into the existing Abyssinian gene pool in the USA. The Abyssinian has become one of the most popular shorthair breed of cats in the USA. There are said to still be wild Abyssinians in some parts of North Africa.

The Abyssinian has a distinctly ticked, tawny coat. The tail and paws may show tabby markings, but the body must not. It has large almond-shaped green or gold eyes with a fine dark line around them, and large ears. The coat is generally a warm golden colour, but "Abys" can also be blue, fawn, cinnamon and red. There is also a Silver Abyssinian variant whose coat shows shades of white, cream and grey. Abyssinians are very active, friendly, curious and playful, but are usually not "lap cats", being too preoccupied with exploring and playing. They are "busy" cats, and can get bored and depressed without daily activity and attention. Many Abyssinians enjoy heights, and will explore their surroundings in three dimensions, from the floor to their owner's shoulders to the top of the highest furniture. They are highly intelligent, and probably the most independent of any domestic breed.

AMERICAN BOBTAIL

The American Bobtail is most notable for its stubby "bobbed" tail about one-third to one-half the length of a normal cat's tail. This is the result of a genetic mutation affecting the tail development, similar to that of a Manx. The cat is not related to the Japanese Bobtail despite the similar name and physical type — the breeding programs are entirely unrelated and the gene causing the mutation is entirely different. American bobtails are a very sturdy breed, with both short or longhaired coats. Their coat is shaggy rather than dense or fluffy. They can have any colour of eyes and fur, with a strong emphasis on the "wild" tabby appearance in show animals. According to legend, bobtails are the result of a crossbreeding between a domestic tabby cat and a bobcat. Yodie, a short-tailed brown tabby male, mated with a seal point Siamese (cat) female to create the Bobtail's original bloodline. Then Birman, Himalayan (cat) and Himalayan/Siamese cross elements were added to the bloodline. Most of the early bloodlines have been eliminated. Although this is genetically possible, the bobcat/domestic cat hybrids, particularly the male, would probably become sterile. The unusual tail is actually the result of a random spontaneous genetic mutation within the domestic cat population or is related to the dominant Manx gene. This cat's original appearance genetics were modified in the breed to form a new and improved breed which comes in all colors, categories and divisions. New shorthair versions have appeared where once only longhair versions were fully recognized. These new lines, which invoke a gentler sweeter cat with the remaining wild look features, may have begun in Florida. It is still permitted to outcross the Bobtail with domestic stock, so long as the currently small gene pool is kept healthy.

AMERICAN CURL

The American Curl is a breed of cat characterized by its unusual ears, which curl back from the face toward the center of the back of the skull. The breed originated in Lakewood, California as the result of a spontaneous mutation. In June, 1981, two stray kittens were found and taken in by the Ruga family. The kittens were both longhaired, one black and the other black and white. The family named them Shulamith and Panda respectively, but Panda disappeared several weeks later, making Shulamith the foundation female of the American Curl breed. In 1983, an American Curl was exhibited at a cat show for the first time, and in 1987, the longhaired American Curl was given championship status by The International Cat Association (TICA). In 1993, the American Curl became the first breed admitted to the Cat Fanciers' Association (CFA) Championship Class with both longhair and shorthair divisions . The American Curl is a medium sized cat (5-10 lbs), and does not reach maturity until 2-3 years of age. They are strong and healthy, remarkably free of the genetic defects that affect many purebred cats. American Curl kittens are born with straight ears, which begin to curl within ten days. After four months, their ears will not curl any longer, and should be hard and stiff to the touch. A pet quality American Curl may have almost straight ears, but showcats must have ears that curl in an arc between 90 and 180 degrees. A greater angle is preferable, but cats will be disqualified if their ears touch the back of their skulls. Both longhaired and shorthaired American Curls have soft, silky coats which lie flat against their bodies. They require little grooming, but enjoy spending time with their owners. The American Curl, while still an uncommon breed, is found across the world in the United States, Spain, France, Japan, Russia, and many other countries.

AMERICAN SHORTHAIR

The American Shorthair is the most popular and most prevalent breed. The breed is believed to be descended from English cats (the forebears of today's British Shorthairs) brought to North America by early European settlers to protect valuable cargo from mice and rats. American Shorthairs are medium to large sized cats, with powerful legs and strong paws. Their muzzle is squarish. Their coat is short, with the fur being thick, dense, and stiff to protect them from cold, moisture, and superficial skin injuries. Their coat thickens up in the winter and sheds in the spring but still remains lighter and slimmer than its close cousin, the British Shorthair. American Shorthairs are very affectionate, long-living, and disinclined to behavioral problems; they get along well with other family members, including dogs. The American Shorthair is also an excellent hunter, but its sunny and gentle disposition make it ideal for families with small children. Shorthairs tend to get overweight very easily. An American Shorthair is not considered fully grown until 3-4 years old, when it attains the true strong athletic proportion of its breed. Males are usually larger than females and whole males have definite jowls. It is perfectly happy as an indoor or outdoor cat. American Shorthairs come in over 100 different varieties of colors (blacks, whites, silvers, creams, reds, browns, blues, bicolors, tabby or solid), but their eyes, pad color, and nose will always match their coloring. Their tail tapers to a blunt tip and has no kinks. Grooming for an American Shorthair is extremely easy, all they require is regular brushing and a wipe over with a damp chamois will make the coat shine.

BALINESE

The Balinese is a breed of oriental cat with long hair and Siamese-style markings, or points. They resemble a Siamese with a medium-length silky coat and a plumed tail, but not nearly as fluffy as a Himalayan, and they require much less grooming. The occasional long-haired kittens in a Siamese litter were seen as an oddity, and sold as household pets rather than as show cats. This changed in the mid-1950s, when two breeders, Mrs. Marion Dorsey and Mrs. Helen Smith decided that they would commence a breeding program for the longhaired cats. Helen Smith named the cats 'Balinese' because she felt they showed the grace and beauty of Balinese dancers. Like the Siamese, there are now two different varieties of Balinese being bred and shown - 'traditional' Balinese and 'contemporary' Balinese. The traditional Balinese cat has a coat approximately two inches long over its entire body and it is a sturdy and robust cat with a semi-rounded muzzle and ears. The traditional Balinese closely resembles a Ragdoll cat although they do not share any of the same genes or breeding other than having a partially Siamese ancestry. A 'contemporary' Balinese has a much shorter coat and is virtually identical to a standard show Siamese except for its tail, which is a graceful silky plume. In most associations, the Balinese is accepted in a full range of colors, including the four traditional Siamese point colors of seal, blue, chocolate, and lilac, as well as less traditional colors such as red and cream, and patterns such as lynx (tabby) point and tortie point. However, in CFA, the Balinese is only accepted in the four traditional Siamese colors; all other colors and patterns are considered Javanese.

BENGAL

The Bengal is a relatively new hybrid breed of cat, which exhibits the "wild" markings (such as large spots, rosettes, and a light/white belly), and body structure reminiscent of the wild Asian Leopard Cat (Prionailurus bengalensis). The Bengal cat has a desirable "wild" appearance with a gentle domestic cat temperament, provided it is separated by at least three generations from the original crossing between a domestic feline and an Asian Leopard Cat. The name Bengal was derived from the taxonomic name of the Asian Leopard Cat (ALC), as shown above, and not from the more widely known Bengal tiger species, which is unrelated to the Bengal's ancestry. Throughout the 1960s and 1970s there was a great deal of activity with hybrids, but there was no significant effort to create an actual breed from them. A number of Cat clubs formed that oriented on hybrids and a few oriented specifically on something William Engler, a member of the Long Island Ocelot Club and a breeder, called a Bengal.

Club newsletters detailing the production of Bengals and Safaris started being published and members of these clubs bred some second and third generation Bengals. These were registered with the American Cat Fanciers Association (A.C.F.A.) in 1977 as experimental and were shown at several A.C.F.A. cat shows throughout the 1970s. Credit also needs to be given at this point to Greg and Elizabeth Kent, who developed their own line of Bengals using ALCs and Egyptian Maus. This was a very successful line and many modern Bengals will find it in their pedigree. Jean Mills and the Kents worked hard to popularize the breed, and when the public saw the result of their work, word spread quickly.

BIRMAN

Birmans have been bred as companions for many generations, and, as such, are very loving. They frequently take a genuine, affectionate interest in what their owners do. Birmans are typically used as show cats who travel with their owners if they are "show quality", meaning that the color of their paws (usually white) and the color of their legs must not blend or intermingle. Birmans are mostly known thanks to their stunning features. The semi-long, silky hair, the cobby body and cute little ears make them very pleasing to look at. The most beautiful thing about a Birman is, however, its colouring. Birmans are all born white (as other colourpoint kittens are) and they start developing their colours at the age of 14 days. The Birman's body ought to be of an eggshell colour or golden, depending on the intensity of the markings colour. The markings can be pure seal, chocolate, blue, red, lilac or cream. Tabby variations are also allowed. Tortie cats can be seal, chocolate, blue or lilac. What is also interesting about the Birmans is their Saphire eyes. The Birman's coat is unusual due to the white 'gloves' on each paw. The white paws are what makes Birmans so special. They are the only cat breed in the colourpoint coat that has fingers and toes in pure white colour. The genetics of this feature is still unclear. Points of Sacred Birman are: Seal-point, Blue-point, Chocolate-point, Lilac-point, Seal Tortie-point, Cream-point, Blue Cream point, Chocolate Tortie point, Lilac Tortie point. Birmans differ from conventional colour-point cats by their white paws called gloves. The coat is medium-length, not as long and thick as a Persian's, and does not mat. Their most striking feature is their clear blue eyes, which remain blue throughout their life.

BOMBAY

The Bombay is a muscular yet agile cat with a black coat. The heads of Bombay cats are rounded and wide with a short tapered muzzle. The eyes, which are of golden or copper color, are rounded and set wide, and their ears are broad, slightly rounded and medium sized and, like the eyes, set wide. The Bombay has a coat that is short, satiny and tight to the body. While Bombay cats will tolerate other breeds of cat, they may tend to dominate other cats. Bombay cats seem to get along well with dogs. Dogs are pack animals and have a pecking order which the Bombay will take advantage of. Like most cats that have been raised properly, Bombay cats are smart, agile and inquisitive. They will often seek out human interaction. Bombay cats are by nature lap cats. They seek heat and will jump up on their owner's backs and rest around their neck for comfort and reassurance. These cats are head-bumpers and nose-rubbers, Some can be very "talkative" (meow loudly) and have distinct "voices". The Bombay will often "fetch", and takes on other dog-like charactaristics. These cats love nothing more than to be held and fussed over. Sensitive, reserved and intelligent, the Bombay is suited to life in a quiet home, where it is affectionate to the whole family. Both males and females are excellent pets. Bombay cats enjoy being around anyone, but may select someone specific to pay the most attention to. they are wonderful for families with children but may be at first annoyed with a new cat in the house. Bombay cats are rumoured to have sometimes unusual diets as lap cats. They may actually eat not just sour cream, but baked cookies or beans if the situation arises. Like many other species of domestic cats, they are rather sneaky and creative at the kitchen table.

BRITISH SHORTHAIR

British Shorthairs have very dense, plush coats that are often described as crisp or cracking which refers to the way the coat breaks over the cat's body contours. Eyes are large, round and copper in colour. British Shorthairs are large and muscular, and are desribed as having a "cobby" build. The breed has a broad chest, shoulders and hips with short legs, round paws and a plush but not fluffy tail. The British Shorthair may be any colour or pattern including all solid colours, dilutes, tabby patterns, bicolours and colourpoints. The typical lifespan of this breed is 9 to 15 years. The British Shorthair is an easygoing breed. It is not normally destructive or hyperactive, although it can be playful. It has become a favorite of animal trainers because of its nature and intelligence, and in recent years these cats have appeared in Hollywood films and television commercials. The British Shorthair does not require a lot of grooming because the fur does not tangle or mat easily. However, it is recommended that the coat be brushed now and again, especially during seasonal shedding. The British Shorthair is prone to obesity especially when desexed or kept indoors. They are also known to have teeth and gum issues, more so than the average cat, so keep their teeth clean with raw bones, chicken wings and dental diets to help control tartar. Writer Lewis Carroll and illustrator Sir John Tenniel chose the breed as the model for the Cheshire cat in Alice's Adventures in Wonderland . A British Shorthair silver tabby is the face of Whiskas and a British Blue is the face of Sheba cat food. In Terry Pratchett's Discworld Humour/Fantasy Novels, the Lancre Witch Nanny Ogg's cat Greebo (also known as The Terror of the Ramtops) is a British Blue. Also Winston Churchill (Church) from Pet Semetary was a British Blue.

BURMESE

Originally, Burmese cats were exclusively brown (sable), but years of selective breeding have produced a wide variety of colours. The Burmese is considered a foreign shorthair. Accepted eye colour for the breed is gold or yellow, although interbreeding with Siamese may lead to blue or green. The coat is known for being glossy, with a satin finish. As with most short-hairs, it requires no additional grooming. The shape of the British breed is more Oriental, while the American breed is sturdier in build. Longer lived than most pedigree cats, they often reach 16 to 18 years of age. The earliest records of the type now known as Burmese come from Thailand, then known as Siam. These cats are thought to have remained in Thailand until it was invaded by the Burmese in the 18th century; returning soldiers may have taken the temple cats with them back to Burma. From about 1949 to 1956, the British Burmese population was being enriched with cats imported from America. The cats which fed the British breeding programme were of a variety of builds. By 1952, three generations had been produced in Britain and official recognition was granted by the Governing Council of the Cat Fancy and the breed was accorded the breed number 27. Until the late 1960s, the gene pool in Britain was very small, with most Burmese being descended from 6 initial imports and a Burmese/Chinese hybrid from Singapore. The controversy stems around the fact that "contemporary" Burmese sometimes carry a lethal head defect and affected kittens do not survive. This problem does not generally occur with "traditional" Burmese. Breeders feel justified in continuing with "contemporary" Burmese because defective kittens die before they are of age to be sold.

CHARTREUX

The Chartreux is an internationally recognized breed from France. Physically, the Chartreux is large and muscular, with short fine-boned limbs, big paws, and very fast reflexes. They have been described as "potatoes on toothpicks". They are known for their blue (grey) water-resistant short hair double-coats and gold- or copper-colored eyes. Chartreux cats are also known for their "smile"; due to the structure of their heads and their long, tapered muzzle, they often appear to be smiling. Chartreux are exceptional hunters and were highly prized by farmers. Chartreux cats tend to be quiet, rarely making noises such as mewing or crying, and some are mute. They are quite observant and intelligent, with some Chartreux learning to operate radio on/off buttons and to open screen door latches. They take about two years to reach adulthood. Chartreux cats are playful cats well into their adult years; some can be taught to fetch small objects in the same manner as a dog. Chartreux are good with children and other animals. Chartreux tend to bond with one person in their household, preferring to be in their general vicinity (often following their person from room to room), though they are still loving and affectionate to the other members of the household. In 1987, the Cat Fanciers' Association (CFA) advanced the Chartreux breed to championship status (Siegal 1997:27). The first letter of the official name of a Chartreux cat encodes the year of its birth; all Chartreux born in the same year have official names beginning with the same letter. The code letters rotate through the alphabet each year, omitting the letters K, Q, W, X, Y, and Z. For example, a Chartreux born in 2002 would have an official name starting with the letter T (Fogle 2001:128).

COLORPOINT SHORTHAIR

Colorpoint Shorthair is the name the Cat Fanciers Association (CFA), uses to refer to pointed cats of Siamese ancestry and type in colors other than the four "traditional" Siamese colors (seal, chocolate, blue, and lilac point). This name is also given to cats of Siamese ancestry in the four recognized colors whose eight generation pedigree show ancestors with other colors.

The Colorpoint Shorthair (a.k.a. Siamese) is a highly intelligent, playful, and people-friendly breed. They are extremely affectionate, outgoing and enjoy lounging around and playing with people. Like their Siamese cousins, Colorpoint Shorthairs require little grooming and are especially good in households with allergies to cats since both breeds have little dander. An occasional bath is recommended, but allow the freshly bathed coat to air dry in a warm spot. Do not blow dry, but do brush the coat with the concave or short side of a small rubber brush to remove loose hair and make the coat lie smooth. The coat can be "finished" by smoothing the coat with a chamois cloth. Balanced diets high in protein are generally recommended, since part of the natural beauty of the Colorpoints is their glistening, muscular hard tubular bodies. Usually breeders make kittens available between twelve and sixteen weeks of age. After twelve weeks, kittens have had their basic inoculations and developed the physical and social stability needed for a new environment, showing, or being transported by air. Keeping such a rare treasure indoors, neutering or spaying and providing acceptable surfaces (e.g. scratching posts) for the natural behavior of scratching (CFA disapproves of declawing or tendonectomy surgery) are essential elements for maintaining a healthy, long and joyful life.

CORNISH REX

A Cornish Rex is a breed of domestic cat. The Cornish Rex has no hair except for down. Most breeds of cat have three different types of hair in their coats: the outer fur or "guard hairs", which is about 5 cm long in shorthairs and 10cm+ long in longhairs; a middle layer called the "awn hair"; and the down hair or undercoat, which is very fine and about 1 cm long. Cornish Rexes only have the undercoat and thus only lose a few of very fine hairs at a time like humans and do not shed like other cats.Some Cornish Rexes also have a mild cheesy smell peculiar to the breed; this odour comes from scent glands in the paws. Some Cornish Rexes like to play fetch, race other pets, or do acrobatic jumps. The Cornish Rex is an adventurous cat and is very intelligent. The Devon Rex looks similar in appearance to the Cornish Rex, but has guard hairs and sheds. The Devon Rex mutation is different than the Cornish Rex mutation in that the Devon has shortened guard hairs, while the Cornish Rex lacks guard hairs altogether. Crosses between Devon and Cornish Rexes are not permitted in pedigrees and matings between them will not produce a cat with short wavy fur. Another hair-deficient breed is the Sphynx cat, which has no hair but may have a very light coat of fuzz. Despite some belief to the contrary, the Cornish Rex's short hair does not make it non- or hypo-allergenic. Most people who have cat allergies are allergic to cat dander and cat saliva. Since Cornish Rex cats groom as much as or even more than ordinary cats, a Cornish Rex cat will still produce a reaction in people who are allergic to cats. Using the word "Rex" to imply short or otherwise unusual fur originates from an occasion when King Albert I of Belgium (1875-1934) entered some short-haired rabbits in a rabbit show.

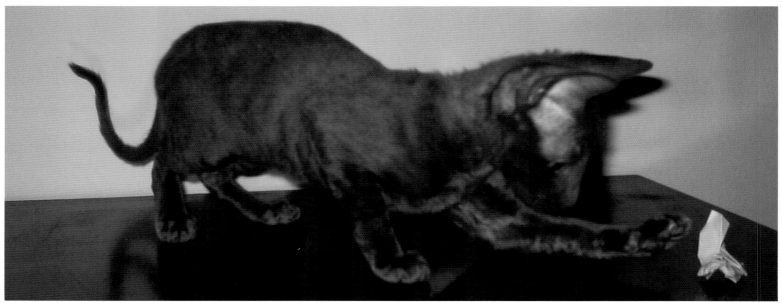

DEVON REX

A very rare and select breed, the average Devon Rex has appreciated in value in the last decade, and a good specimen can fetch a high price. The Devon Rex is a relatively new breed of cat with a sparse, curly, very soft coat similar to that of the Cornish Rex. The first Devon was discovered in Buckfastleigh, Devon, UK in 1960 amongst a litter of feral kittens, and was initially thought to be linked with the Cornish Rex; however, test mating proved otherwise. Cats have three types of hair: guard hair, awn hair, and down hair. The Cornish Rex's coat is unusual because there is no guard hair. In the Devon Rex, all types of hair are present but are abnormal in texture. The curl in Devon Rex fur is caused by a different mutation and gene than that of the Cornish Rex and German Rex, and breeding of a Devon with either of those cats results in cats without rexed (curled) fur. Their uncommonly large ears are set low on the sides of their wide heads, their eyes are large, and their noses are slightly upturned. Their body type is distinctly lightly-built. Their long, sturdy legs are great for long leaps, and their toes are unusually large. Devon Rex cats come in most colours. The typical Devon is active, mischievous, playful, and very people-oriented. The Devon Rex breed is often marketed as a cat with which someone with cat-related allergies can easily co-exist. It is true that their missing layer of hair and very low amounts of shedding help toward this, but they are not hypoallergenic. However, they are easier for someone on the right allergy medication to own.

EGYPTIAN MAU

Egyptian Maus are a medium-sized short-haired cat breed. Egyptian Maus are the fastest breed of domestic cat, capable of running at 36 mph. Males are usually somewhat larger than females. The longer hind legs are another reason for the breed's startling speed. The Mau also has a loose flap of skin on the lower abdomen, similar to the cheetah, which allows a longer stride while running, again contributing to its great speed. They have anatomical, metabolic and behavioral differences from other cat breeds which could be considered as evidence of antiquity or at least uniqueness from other cat breeds. Besides those already mentioned, Maus are more temperature sensitive than most breeds - they are fond of very warm temperatures. Maus also have an unusually long gestational period. The maximum normal period for cats is 69 days, although Siamese may take a day or two longer. For a Mau, 73 days is still considered normal. Maus often possess very musical voices. They are known to chirp, chortle and emit other distinctly unusual vocalizations when stimulated. Purebred Egyptian Maus are a relatively rare breed. Currently, the number of registered Egyptian Maus worldwide is probably about 3000. Maus are such a rare breed some animal shelters will not take them in, but pass them directly to Mau breed rescue leagues. Maus come in five colors. Three can be shown: silver, smoke and bronze. Black and pewter Maus cannot be shown, but can be used in breeding. All Maus must have green eyes, but an amber cast is acceptable in kittens and young adults up to eighteen months old. In the 2004 movie Catwoman, the cat 'Midnight' who brought Patience Phillips back to life as Catwoman was played by three Egyptian Maus, as well as a computer-generated Mau.

EUROPEAN SHORTHAIR

European Shorthair has its counterparts in Great Britain (British Shorthair)and USA (American Shorthair), that have been bred much longer. The British Shorthair however was crossed with Persian Cat and selectively bred to become a cobbier cat with slightly shortened muzzle and thicker coat. It was confusing for Scandinavian breeders that BS was also called European Shorthair at that time, even though it looked differently. Felinological associations recognized both types of cats as a single breed so that they were judged by the same standards during cat shows. It was so until 1982 when FIFE registered the Scandinavian type of European Shorthair as a separate breed with its own standard. Members of this breed may be very affectionate but there are others that prefer to be out mousing. Most European Shorthairs are strong and healthy, and as a rule they are friendly. European Shorthairs are intelligent and playful, and most of them are expert at keeping houses and gardens free of mice. The European Shorthair is a muscular, medium-sized to large cat, with a broad, well-muscled chest. The strong legs are average length and the paws are round. The tail is fairly thick at the base, tapering to a rounded point. The relatively large head is rounded, with well-developed jowls, but it is not as round as the British Shorthair's head. The ears are medium-sized, they are as long as they are broad at the base, with slightly rounded tip. They are quite wide-set and upright. The eyes are round and may be of any colour. The European Shorthair's dense coat is short, soft and glossy, and should lie flat. All natural colours are permitted, such as black, red, blue and cream, with or without tabby or white markings. Pure white is also permitted. The eye colour corresponds to the coat colour and may be yellow, green or orange.

EXOTIC

Breeders crossed the American Shorthair with the Persian in the United States around 1960. Thus were born shorthaired Persians, called Exotic Shorthairs and recognized by the C.F.A in 1966. During the breeding program, crosses were also made with the Russian Blue and the Burmese. Since 1987, the only allowable outcross breed is the Persian. The F.I.Fe. recognized the Exotic Shorthair in 1986. They have nearly the same body as the Persian, but a thick, dense short coat. They appeal to people who like the personality of a Persian but do not want the hassle of grooming a long-haired cat. They are also known as "The Lazy Man's Persian"

The Exotic has a compact, rounded, powerfully-built body with a short, thick "linebacker" neck. Its large round eyes, short snub nose, sweet facial expression, and small ears give it a highly neotenic appearance that many people consider cute.

The Exotic Shorthair has a gentle and calm personality reminiscent of the Persian, but he is livelier than his longhaired ancestor. Curious and playful, he is friendly to other cats and dogs. Easygoing and quiet, as he rarely meows. He doesn't like being left alone, he needs the presence of his owner, but he's always independent. They tend to show more affection and loyalty than most breeds and make excellent lap cats. Their calm and steady nature makes them ideal apartment cats for city dwellers. Nonetheless, Exotics retain some of the energetic spark of their American Shorthair forbears and they are often capable mouse hunters.

JAPANESE BOBTAIL

The Japanese Bobtail is a breed of cat with an unusual 'bobbed' tail more closely resembling the tail of a rabbit than that of an ordinary feline. The short tail is caused by the expression of a recessive gene. Thus, so long as both parents are bobtails, all kittens born to a litter will have bobtails as well. Unlike the Manx and other cat breeds, where genetic disorders are common to tailless or stumpy-tails, no such problem exists with the Japanese Bobtail. The breed is a small domestic cat native to Japan and Southeast Asia. The breed has been known in Japan for centuries, and there are many legends and myths, as well as pieces of ancient art, featuring it. Japanese bobtails may have almost any color, but "Mi-ke" or bi-colors are especially favoured by the Japanese. Much like any other breed, the colors may be arranged in any number of patterns, with van and calico being common among purebred cats and tabby being seen in non-purebred Japanese bobtails. They usually have litters of three to four kittens with newborns that are unusually large compared to other breeds. They are active earlier, and walk earlier. Affectionate and generally sweet-tempered, they enjoy supervising household chores and baby-sitting. They are active, intelligent, talkative cats with a well-defined sense of family life. Their soft voices are capable of nearly a whole scale of tones; some people say they sing. Since they adore human companionship they almost always speak when spoken to. Because of their human-oriented personality they are easy to teach tricks and enjoy learning things like walking on a harness and lead.

KORAT

The Korat is one of the oldest stable breeds of cat. Originating in Thailand, it is named after the Nakhon Ratchasima province, although in Thailand it is often known as Si-Sawat, which means good fortune. In fact they are often known colloquially as the "Good Luck Cat" and are given in pairs to newlyweds or people of high esteem as a wish for good luck.

Korats have extraordinary powers of hearing, sight and scent. They are gentle pets, moving softly and cautiously, disliking sudden, loud or harsh noises. Those destined to be shown must be trained from birth to accept noise and handling, possibly by keeping a radio on in the nursery, and by lifting and posing the kitten as judges do. Korats form an exceptionally strong bond of affection with their owners and respond warmly to cuddling, setting as close as possible. They mix well with other cats but tend to want to have the upper hand and will not let the others keep them from their rightful place at their owner's side. They have been cherished for centuries in their native Thailand and they naturally expect this tradition to be maintained wherever they go. Korats are active in their play, but are very gentle with children. The first known written mention of the Korat was in "The Cat-Book Poems" authored between 1350 and 1767 AD in Thailand, now preserved in the National library in Bangkok. They first appeared in America in the 1950s and arrived in Britain from there in 1972. Korats are a shorthair with a small to medium build and a low percentage of body fat; their bodies are often described as semi-cobby, and are surprisingly heavy for their size. They are an active cat and form strong bonds with people.

KURILIAN BOBTAIL

The Kurilian Bobtail is a compact and strongly muscled cat similar to, though larger than, the Japanese Bobtail. It is unfortunate that two recently recognised bobtail breeds (the Karelian of east Russia and the Kurilian which originates off the coast of west Russia) were not only discovered in a similar time frame and both developed by Russian breeders, but a similarity in their names has also fanned an confusion about their difference from the Japanese Bobtail. People tend to see only the cats' gross similarity - most specifically their corkscrew 'pom pom' tail. Perhaps, given the visual similarity in tails, it can be understood why the acceptance of either breed has become tangled in the notion that these cats are just the Japanese Bobtail by another name. Yet while the Karelian is slender the Kurilian is a completely distinct breed with a different body type than either the Karelian or the Japanese Bobtail.The Kurilian has been recognised as a distinct breed by WCF and SFF, and will soon be considered by FIFe. A comparison between the standards of the Kurilian Bobtail and the Japananese Bobtail demonstrates why they are not considered the same breed.Please note that I have double-checked these points with my Russian breed mentor, Svetlana Ponomareva. She is president of a Russian breed club & a breeder of Persian, Kurilian & American Curl who has also worked with Scottish Folds & Exotics and WCF Judge Shorthair Group. I have also checked my points with Lisa Rowe, a breeder of Japanese Bobtails in the USA.

LA PERM

A LaPerm's fur is curly (hence the name "perm"), with the tightest curls being on the belly, throat and base of the ears. La Perms come in many colours and patterns. The LaPerm is a rex breed from the USA whose popularity has increased worldwide steadily since it was introduced. These cats are genetically unique and not related to any other rex breeds, having a dominant gene causing their curly coats. They have an elegant and athletic build and are affectionate, active and outgoing in character. Their most significant feature is their coat which is made up of soft waves, curls and ringlets, resembling a shaggy perm.

The first LaPerm was born in 1982 and was a spontaneous mutation in an otherwise normal litter of kittens born on Linda and Richard Koehl's cherry farm in The Dalles, Oregon under a tree in the middle of a rainstorm one night. Linda heard strange noises and took a torch outside to find Curly the mother fiercely staving off barking dogs while straddling her newborn babies. All five were male and grew up to have the same soft curls. None of the five were neutered and their breeding activity led to many more curly coated kittens being born. Linda found herself with a growing colony of unusual rex cats which included long and short coats and (thanks to the input somewhere along the way of a local cat who had a Siamese mother) chocolate and colourpoints too. It was only when people started commenting on her odd cats and asking what they were that she did some research and realised that she had some kind of rex. She took some cats to a show to ask for feedback and was told by exhibitors, breeders and judges that she had something very special. Cat fancies gave her their support and the breed has grown and to become a well established championship breed with breeding programmes around the world.

 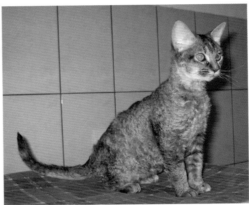 

MAINE COON

The Maine Coon breed is one of the oldest natural breeds in North America and originated from New England, making it America's first indigenous show cat. The Maine Coon Cat is known as "the gentle giant." Maine Coons are similar in appearance to both the Norwegian Forest Cat and to the Siberian. Maine Coons are very large and energetic cats, sometimes weighing up to around 11-12 kilograms (25 pounds); the average weight is 6 to 9 kilograms (13-20 pounds) for adult males and less (7-11 pounds) for females. Male Maine Coons may grow to a length in excess of 1 meter (40 inches); the longest cat on record is a Maine Coon 121cm (49 inches) in length. Growth to full size often takes longer than for most cats, with Maine Coons usually reaching full size at age four or five. The most common color/pattern in the breed is brown with tabby markings. Maine Coons are recognized in all colors, including tortoiseshell, except for chocolate, lavender, ticked tabby, and the point-restricted ("Siamese") pattern. Eye color also varies widely. All patterns may have green, green-gold, or gold. Blue eyes, or one blue eye with one gold eye, are possible in white coat cats. They share similar facial markings, for example, a distinct "M" shape on the forehead Maine Coons have medium-long, dense fur, with longer hair, or a ruff, on their chests similar to the mane of a lion (which is why the breed is sometimes humorously called the "Mane Coon"). Their fur consists of two layers - an undercoat and an additional layer of longer guard hairs, which gives the breed their key physical feature.

MANX

The Manx is a breed of cats with a naturally occurring mutation of the spine. This mutation shortens the tail, resulting in a range of tail lengths from normal to tailless. Many Manx have a small 'stub' of a tail, but Manx cats are best known as being entirely tailless and it is the distinguishing characteristic of the breed. The Manx breed originated on the Isle of Man (hence the name), where they are common. The taillessness arises from a genetic mutation that became common on the island. The Manx tailless gene is dominant and highly penetrant; kittens from Manx parents are generally born without any tail. Having two copies of the gene is lethal and kittens are usually spontaneously aborted before birth. This means that tailless cats can carry only one copy of the gene.

Manx cats exhibit two coat lengths. The short-haired Manx has a double coat with a thick, short under-layer and a longer, coarse outer-layer with guard hairs. The long-haired Manx, known to some cat registries as the Cymric, has a silky-textured double coat of medium length, with britches, belly and neck ruff, tufts of fur between the toes and full ear furnishings. The Manx breed is a highly intelligent cat breed, and as such is extremely playful. Manx behavior can seem bizarre, and very reminiscent of dogs; for example, some Manx cats will fetch small objects that are thrown. They will walk well on leashes, enjoy going outdoors and riding in cars. It is considered a social feline, and the breed loves humans, they need a lot of attention and leaving one alone for too long can be cruel. This attribute makes them an ideal breed for families with young children and people who prefer a companion.

NORWEGIAN FOREST CAT

The Norwegian Forest Cat is a breed of domestic cat native to Northern Europe, and adapted to a very cold climate. In Norway they are known as Skogkatter or Skaukatter (skog and skau being forms of the word for 'forest' in different Norwegian dialects) or more properly, the Norsk Skogkatt (literally, Norwegian Forest Cat). The breed is very old, and occurred as a natural adaptation to the cold climate of the region, but it was not regarded as anything other than a standard house-cat until the late 1930s, when a small number of 'Skaukatts' were shown in Germany and received very favourably by the judges. World War II brought an abrupt end to the fledgling Norwegian show cat industry, and the breed was forgotten until the 1970s. The cats are now being bred and shown in several countries including the United States.

Norwegian Forest Cats have a thick fluffy double-layered coat, tufted ears and a long bushy tail to protect them against the cold. Their coat is essentially waterproof due to its coarse outer layer and dense underlay. They are very large cats with adult males weighing 6 to 10 kg (13 to 22 lb), while females are approximately half that size. Their hind legs are longer than their front legs. They are very intelligent, playful cats that enjoy human company. The nickname of "Wegie" began in the United States and is a shortened version of the word Norwegian. Like Maine Coons, Norwegian Forest Cats are an intelligent, robust and playful breed. They like the outdoors, are well suited to cold conditions and are great hunters. Despite their great affection for the outdoors, however, they also enjoy the company of humans and other pets and will sometimes go looking for company if left alone by their owners.

OCICAT

The Ocicat is a new and still-rare breed of cat which has spots resembling a 'wild' cat and the temperament of a domestic animal, named for its resemblance to the ocelot. Despite its appearance, there is no 'wild' DNA in the Ocicat's gene pool. The species is actually a mixture of Siamese and Abyssinian, and later American Shorthairs (silver tabbies) were added to the mix and gave the breed their silver colour, bone structure and distinct markings.

The first breeder of Ocicats was Virginia Daly, of Berkley, Michigan, who attempted to breed an Abyssinian-pointed Siamese in 1964. The first generation of kittens appeared Abyssinian, but the surprising result in the second generation was a spotted kitten, Tonga, nicknamed an 'ocicat' by the breeder's daughter. Tonga was neutered and sold as a pet, but further breedings of his parents produced more spotted kittens, and became the base of a separate Ocicat breeding program. Other breeders joined in and used the same recipe. Today the ocicat is found all around the world, popular for its temperament but wild appearance. Ocicats are a very outgoing breed. They are often considered to have the spirit of a dog-in a cat's body. Most can easily be trained to fetch, walk on a leash and harness, come when called, speak, sit, lie down on command and a large array of other dog-related tricks. Some even take readily to the water. Ocicats are also very friendly. They will typically march straight up to strangers and announce that they'd like to be petted. This makes them great family pets, and most can also get along well with animals of other species. Ocicats make excellent pets for people who want to spend a lot of time with their cat, but they do require more attention than cats who aren't so people-oriented.

ORIENTAL

The Oriental Shorthair is a breed of cat. It is also called a "Foreign Type" cat. This cat combines the Siamese body with a diversity of colorings and patterns. Oriental Shorthairs are intelligent, social animals who bond closely to their people. They are inquisitive, friendly, emotional, demanding and often quite vocal. Oriental Shorthairs have been likened to a Greyhound or a Chihuahua in appearance. Some people say they are 'dog-like' in personality, particularly because they become so attached to people. The Oriental Shorthair is a self-coloured (non-pointed) member of the Siamese Family. They can be found in solid colors (white, red, cream, ebony, blue, chestnut, lavender, cinnamon, or fawn), smoke (white undercoat to any of the above except white), shaded (only the hair tips colored), parti-color (red or cream splashes on any of the above), tabby (mackerel/striped, ticked, spotted, and blotched/classic), and bi-colored (any of the above, with white).

Oriental Shorthairs have expressive, almond-shaped eyes, a wedge-shaped head with large ears that fit in the wedge of the head. Their bodies are very elegant yet muscular. When seeing an Oriental Shorthair, one would never guess them to be as solid as they are. The longhaired version of the Oriental Shorthair, Oriental Longhair, simply carries a pair of the recessive long hair gene. The Siamese cat was imported to Britain from Siam (Thailand) in the later half of the 1800s. According to reports, both pointed and solid colors were imported. Other breeds that were developed from the moggies of Siam include the Havana Brown and the Korat.

PERSIAN

The Persian cat is one of the oldest breeds of cat. In Britain, it is called the "Longhair" or "Persian Longhair". A Persian cat without an established and registered pedigree is classed as a domestic longhair cat. The Persian cat originates from the Iranian plateau, a large area between the Hindukush mountains and Mesopotamia traditionally known as "Persia" in the West. However, interbreeding of Angoras with native British domestic longhairs in the 19th Century makes the true origin of the breed unclear. The Persian's European debut is credited to Pietro Della Valle, an Italian traveller.

A show-quality Persian has an extremely long thick coat, short legs, a wide head with the ears set far apart, large eyes, and an extremely foreshortened muzzle. The breed was originally established with a short (but not non-existent) muzzle, but over time this feature has become extremely exaggerated, particularly in North America, and Persians with the more extreme brachycelphalic head type are prone to a number of health problems (specifically affecting their sinuses and breathing) caused by it. Persian cats can have any color or markings including pointed, tortoiseshell, blue, and tabby. Tipped varieties are known as Chinchilla. Point varieties are called Himalayan in the United States and Colourpoint Persian in Europe.

Because their fur is too long and dense for them to maintain themselves, Persian cats need regular grooming. To keep their fur in its best condition, they must be bathed regularly, dried carefully afterwards, and brushed thoroughly every day. Their eyes need to be checked for problems on a regular basis because some animals have trouble keeping them clean. Longevity is usually between 10 and 18 years on average.

RAGAMUFFIN

The Ragamuffin is a long-haired domestic cat similar in appearance to the Ragdoll. Ragamuffins are large, muscular, heavy cats that do not reach full maturity until approximately four years old. The look of the body is rectangular, with broad chest and powerful shoulders supporting a short neck. The Ragamuffin often has a fatty pad in the lower abdomen. The head is a broad modified wedge with a rounded forehead and obvious nose dip. There is a puffiness to the whisker pad and cheeks are full. Large, walnut shaped eyes give a sweet appearance. The Ragamuffin has a long, dense and silky coat, like that of a heavily furred rabbit, and the hair grows longer around the face and neck (a ruff), increases in length toward the stomach, with a wispy frill on the hind legs. The Ragamuffin is one of the newest breeds of domestic cat. It was created in 1994. The exact development of this breed is cloudy and will likely remain a mystery.

This breed has several of the color formations that are present on Ragdolls, but also has a variety of different colors. Some colors include: all variations of pointed color, including Tortie Point, Red Point, and Lynx Point. The only extreme allowed in this breed is the very docile nature. The Ragamuffin loves people and is very cuddly and affectionate, with a tendency to go limp when held. While not terribly athletic, they love playing and climbing scratching posts and some will even fetch toys. They greet family members at the door and will follow their people around the house. Though some have been known to bite when not given the desired attention. Because of their gentle nature, Ragamuffins are generally kept indoors for their own protection.

RAGDOLL

The Ragdoll is a breed of medium longhaired cat. It is best known for its docile and placid temperament and affectionate nature. They are non-aggressive to the point that many cats cannot or should not be let outside for prolonged periods as many will not defend themselves and most do not hunt. The name "Ragdoll" derived from the fact that many of these cats go completely limp and relax when picked up. Ragdolls have a sturdy body, short legs, and a thick coat with Siamese-style points. Ragdolls were developed in the 1960's by Ann Baker, a Persian breeder in California, some of whose original stock consisted of sturdy, free-roaming cats. It is thought she created the foundations of the Ragdoll breed by selecting kittens out of Josephine, a semi-feral longhaired white female Persian/Angora type, sired by several unknown male Birman-like or Burmese-like cats, one with Siamese markings.

By selecting individuals with the look and temperament she wanted for her breeding program, Ann Baker created the standard Ragdoll type. Denny and Laura Dayton are credited with refining the Ragdoll type and bringing the Ragdoll breed to worldwide recognition by various cat registration organizations. What is known is that this breed was selectively bred over many years for desirable traits, such as large size, gentle demeanor, and a tendency to go limp when picked up. The Ragdoll is a large, semi-longhaired cat, exhibiting the pointed pattern in three varieties: colorpoint (no white), bicolor (white blaze on face, white legs and feet), and mitted (white chin and paws). Point colors can be seal, blue, chocolate, red (flame), lilac and cream. Ragdolls' low shedding, semi-long rabbit-like coats need minimal care and do not usually become matted with regular combing.

RUSSIAN

The Russian Blue has a lean medium-sized body and a short, plush, blue coat. The colour is a blueish-gray that is the dilute expression of the black gene. The coat is unique to the breed as it is a double coat, with the undercoat being soft and downy, and the longer guard hairs an even blue with silver tips. This "tipping" gives the coat a shimmering appearance. Its eyes are green and ideally should be dark and vivid. Common imperfections include yellow eyes, white patches on the underside and dark banding on the tail. These cats are highly intelligent and playful but tend to be shy around strangers. They also develop a close bond with their human companions.

Unlike many modern cat breeds, the Russian Blue is a naturally occurring breed which is believed to have originated in the port of Arkhangelsk, Russia (hence the name), although the evidence for this is purely anecdotal. They are also sometimes called Archangel Blues. During and following World War II, due to a lack of numbers of Russian Blues, some cross breeding with the Siamese breed was introduced. The Siamese traits have now been largely bred out. The majority of their modern breeding program has been carried out in the United States. Although they have been used on a limited basis to create other breeds (such as the Havana Brown) or add type to a breed in creation (the Nebelung), Russian Blues themselves are shorthaired, blue cats. Russian Blues should not be confused with 'British Blues' (which are not a distinct breed but rather a British Shorthair with a blue coat), nor the Chartreux or Korat which are two other naturally occurring breeds of blue cats.

SCOTTISH FOLD

The Scottish Fold—sometimes called Coupari by Canadian breeders—is a breed of cat with a natural dominant-gene mutation that makes its ear cartilage contain a fold, causing the ears to bend forward and down towards the front of their head, which gives the cat what is often described as an "owl-like" appearance. Originally called Flops (for "floppy" ears), the name Scottish Fold became the breed's name in 1966. Longhaired Scottish Folds have various official names depending on the certifying agency, being known as the Highland Fold by the ACFA, AACE, and UFO, Scottish Fold Longhair by the TICA, NCFA, ACA, CCA, and CFA, and Longhair Fold by the CFF.

The original Scottish Fold was a white barn cat named Susie, who was found at a farm near Coupar Angus in Perthshire, Scotland, in 1961. Susie's ears had an unusual fold in their middle, making her resemble an owl. When Susie had kittens, two of them were born with folded ears, and one was acquired by William Ross, a neighbouring farmer and cat-fancier. Ross registered the breed with the Governing Council of the Cat Fancy in Great Britain and started to breed Scottish Fold kittens with the help of geneticist Pat Turner. The breeding program produced 76 kittens in the first three years – 42 with folded ears and 34 with straight ears. The conclusion from this was that the ear mutation is due to a simple dominant gene; if one parent provides the gene for straight ears, and one parent provides the gene for folded ears, the kittens will be Folds. Susie's only reproducing offspring was a female Fold named Snooks who was also white; a second kitten was neutered shortly after birth. Three months after Snooks' birth, Susie was killed by a car.

SELKIRK REX

The Selkirk Rex is a breed of cat with highly curled hair, including the whiskers (vibrissae). Unlike the Devon Rex and Cornish Rex, the hair is of normal length and not partly missing, and there are longhair and shorthair varieties. Also unlike the other Rexes, the Selkirk gene is dominant. The Selkirk Rex originated in Montana, America in 1987, with a litter born to a rescued cat. The only unusually coated kitten in the litter was ultimately placed with a Persian breeder, Jeri Newman, who named her Miss DePesto (after a curly-haired character in the TV series Moonlighting). This foundation cat was bred to a black Persian male, producing three Selkirk Rex and three straight-haired kittens. This demonstrated that the gene had an autosomal dominant mode of inheritance. All Selkirk Rex trace their ancestry back to Miss DePesto.

The breed has been developed in two coat lengths, long and short (medium). It is a large and solidly built breed, similar to a British Shorthair. The coat is very soft and has a woolly look and feel with loose, unstructured curls. The head is round, with large rounded eyes, medium sized ears, and a distinct muzzle, whose length is equal to half its width. An extreme break, like that of a Persian, is a disqualifiable fault. This breed has an extremely dense coat and high propensity for shedding. Unlike other Rex breeds with reduced amounts of hair, the Selkirk Rex is not recommended for those who might be allergic to cat allergens. The temperament of the Selkirk Rex reflects that of the breeds used in its development. They have a lot of the laid-back, reserved qualities of the British Shorthair, the cuddly nature of the Persian, and the playfulness of the Exotic Shorthair. They are very patient, tolerant, and loving.

SIAMESE

The Siamese is one of the first distinctly recognised breeds of Oriental cat. The exact origins of the breed are unknown, but it is believed to be from Southeast Asia, and is said to be descended from the sacred temple cats of Siam (now Thailand). In Thailand, where they are one of several native breeds, they are called Wichien-maat (a name meaning "Moon diamond"). All Siamese have a creamy base coat with coloured points on their snouts, ears, paws and lower legs, tails and (in males) scrota. The pointed pattern is a form of partial albinism, resulting from a mutation in tyrosinase, an enzyme involved in melanin production. The mutated enzyme is heat-sensitive; it fails to work at normal body temperatures, but becomes active in cooler areas of the skin. This results in dark colouration in the coolest parts of the cat's body, including the extremities and the face, which is cooled by the passage of air through the sinuses. All Siamese kittens, although pure cream or white at birth, develop visible points in the first few months of life in colder parts of their body. Siamese have almond-shaped, bright blue eyes and short, flat-lying coats. Siamese are affectionate and intelligent cats, renowned for their social nature. They enjoy being with people and are sometimes described as "extroverts". They are extremely vocal, with a loud, low-pitched voice that has been compared to the cries of a human baby, and persistent in demanding attention. They also have a great need for human companionship. Often they bond strongly to a single person. These cats are typically active and playful, even as adults. The social orientation of Siamese cats may be related to their lessened ability to live independently of humans. Siamese coat colouration is appealing to humans, but is ineffective for camouflage purposes.

SIBERIAN

The Siberian is a recognized breed of cat, with most cat organizations accepting Siberians of any color (including color points) for competition. This includes recognition in the major cat registries such as TICA and Cat Fanciers' Association (CFA), as well as acceptance in the CFA Championship class beginning on February 6th, 2006. Known to be an exceptionally high jumper, the Siberian is a strong and powerfully built cat, with well proportioned characteristics that include strong hindquarters and large stomachs. They typically weigh between 15-20 (6.8-9.1 kg) pounds for the males, or 10-15 pounds (4.5-6.8 kg) for females. They are shorter and stockier than Maine Coon cats and Norwegian Forest Cats even though they can attain approximately the same weight. Also, Siberians typically attain their full growth more slowly, over their first 5 years. Siberians are generally intelligent, playful, affectionate and loyal, leading many to describe their character as dog-like. Their fur is plush, can have a wide range of coloration (including points), and does not have a tendency to mat. Siberians may be 90% hypoallergenic. No conclusive information is currently available. Despite the lack of scientific evidence, extensive anecdotal evidence can be found from breeders and pet owners supporting such claims. Siberian fur is textured, medium-long and usually tabby patterned. While Siberians are a fairly recent introduction to the US(1990) and thus relatively rare, though popular, the breed can be seen in Russian paintings and writings hundreds of years old. This sets them apart from breeds that are the result of fairly recent selective breeding. There is an increasing interest in Siberians worldwide, and they are currently accepted in all registries.

SINGAPURA

The Singapura is an alert, healthy, small cat of foreign type. The body has good bone structure and is moderately stocky and muscular, yet gives an impression of great elegance. Females are usually smaller than the males, but still feel heavier than they look. The strong slender legs taper to small oval feet. The tail should be slender but not whippy. and should have a blunt tip. Body colour is an old or golden ivory with a soft warm effect, ticked with sepia brown. Each hair has at least two bands of sepia brown ticking, separated by light bands — light next to skin, and dark tip. Muzzle, chest, stomach and inner legs are an unticked light ivory colour. Singapuras should have some barring on their inner front legs and back knees. The coat is short, fine, silky, and close-lying.

The original home of the Singapura is the island of Singapore, with the breed taking its name from the local Malay name for the island — meaning 'Lion City'. The breed has noticeably large eyes and ears. Eyes are large, set not less than an eye width apart, held wide open, but showing slant when closed or partially closed. A dark outline to the eyes is desirable. Eye colour hazel, green or yellow only. Ears are large, wide open at base, and deep cupped. The outer line of the ears extends upwards to an angle slightly wide of parallel. The head is gently rounded with a definite whisker break and a medium short, broad muzzle with a blunt nose. In profile, the Singapura has a rounded skull with a slight stop just below eye level. There must be evidence of dark pigment outline on the nose. 'Cheetah' lines from the inner corner of the eye towards just behind the whisker pad should be present.

SOMALI

The Somali is a long-haired abyssinian. The breed appeared spontaneously in the 1950s from Abyssinian breeding programs when a number of Abyssinian kittens were born with bottle-brush tails and long fluffy coats. Abyssinians and Somalis share the same personality (active, intelligent, playful, curious) and appearance. The only difference between them is the fur length and therefore the amount of grooming required. Unlike most long-haired cats, Somalis shed very little excess hair. Their coat is generally shed en masse, or "blown", once or twice a year, rather than constantly shedding like a Persian or other long-haired cat. Somalis have a striking, bushy tail, which, combined with their ruddy coat, has earned them the nickname of "fox cats" in some circles. In addition to the fluffy tail, the Somali breed features a black stripe down its back, large ears, a full ruff and breeches, contributing further to the overall "foxy" look. Their coats are ticked, which is a variation on tabby markings, and some Somalis may show full tabby stripes on portions of their bodies, but this is seen as a flaw, and tabby Somalis are only sold as neutered pets. The only tabby marking on a show Somali is the traditional tabby 'M' on the middle of the forehead. Like Abyssinians, they have a dark rim around their eyes that makes them look like they are wearing kohl, and they have a small amount of white on their muzzles and chins/throats. White elsewhere on their bodies disqualifies them from show-status. They are smart and lively, but also alert and curious. They are freedom-loving and must have plenty of room to roam and explore. They are best kept indoors or in outside runs for their own safety. There are four main Somali colors officially accepted within the United States: ruddy, red, blue, and fawn.

SPHYNX

The Sphynx (aka Canadian Hairless) is a rare breed of cat with extremely little fur, or at most a short fuzz over its body, and no, or very short and stiff whiskers (vibrissae). Their skin is the color their fur would be, and all the usual cat marking patterns (solid, point, van, tabby, tortie, etc) may be found in Sphynx too. They are sometimes mistaken for Chihuahuas because of their extremely unusual and, some say, uncatlike appearance. They are extremely intelligent, extroverted, and affectionate, often cuddling with their owners, other humans, and each other.

The Sphynx breed is known for a sturdy, heavy body (many cats of this breed also develop a pot belly), a wedge-shaped head, and an alert, friendly temperament. Other hairless breeds might have different body shapes or temperaments than those described above. There are, for example, new hairless breeds, including the Don Sphynx and the Peterbald from Russia, which arose from their own spontaneous mutations. The standard for the Sphynx differs between TICA and FIFE. Sphynx hairlessness is produced by an allele of the same gene that produces the Cornish Rex, which has only one of the usual two fur coats. The Sphynx allele is incompletely dominant over the Devon allele; both are recessive to the wild type. Sphynx were at one time crossbred with Devon Rex in an attempt to strengthen this gene, but unfortunately this led to serious dental or nervous-system problems and is now forbidden in most breed standards associations. The only allowable outcross breeds in the CFA are now the American Shorthair and Domestic Shorthair. Other associations have different rules. In Europe mainly Devon Rex has been used for outcrosses.

TONKINESE

Tonkinese are a medium-sized short-haired cat breed distinguished by points as with Siamese and Himalayans. They are lively, but are happy apartment cats if have some exercize opportunity. They are commonly referred to as 'Tonks'. As with many cat breeds, the exact history of the Tonkinese varies to some degree depending on the historian. Tonkinese cats are a recent cross between the Siamese and Burmese cat breeds, although some assert that Tonkinese-like cats have existed since at least the early 1800s, and the founding cat of the Burmese breed was probably a mink hybrid-colored cat named "Wong Mau."

Tonkinese cats are commonly trim and muscular cats. They are typically heavier than they appear to be, due to their very muscular bodies. They have a distinctive oval-shaped paw, and a modified wedge-shaped head, with large ears set towards the outside of their head. They are unusually intelligent, curious, affectionate with people, and interested in them. Tonks are playful cats, but not hyperactive, although they can be mischievous if they become lonesome or bored. Some interesting toys and a cat tree, or, better yet, another Tonkinese, will keep them occupied when you're not around. Unlike most breeds of cat, they are reported to sometimes, or even often, engage in fetching, and they can often be found perched on the highest object in the house. They are more like Burmese in temperament than Siamese, that is, less high-strung and demanding. Their voices are also less piercing (or raucous, depending on taste) in most cases than the Siamese, but most Tonks do like a good chat. Most observers feel they combine the more attractive features of both ancestor breeds.

TURKISH ANGORA

Turkish Angoras are one of the ancient, naturally-occurring cat breeds, having originated in central Turkey, in the Ankara region. They mostly have a white, silky, medium-long length coat, no undercoat and fine bone structure. There seems to be a connection between Ankara Cats and Persians (see below), and the Turkish Angora is also a distant cousin of the Turkish Van. Although they are known for their shimmery white coat, currently there are more than twenty varieties including black, blue, reddish fur. They come in tabby and tabby and white, along with smoke varieties, and are in every color other than pointed, lavender, and cinnamon (all of which would indicate breeding to an outcross).

Eyes may be blue, green or amber, but it is often a combination of one blue and one amber. The W gene responsible for white coat and blue eye is closely related to the hearing ability, and presence of a blue eye can indicate the cat is deaf to the side the blue eye is located. However, a great many blue and odd-eyed whites have normal hearing, and even deaf cats lead a very normal, if indoor, life. Ears are pointed and large, and the head is long with a two plane profile. Another characteristic is the tail, which is often kept parallel to the back. Turkish Angora is an intelligent, adorable and very curious breed, very active throughout their life-span. Some Turkish Angoras will bathe with their owners (another link to the cousin Turkish Van cat, which is known as "the swimming cat"). They also tend to bond with their owners and try to be the center of attention, often doing their part in conversations. They usually don't like to be held for long, but like to stay in human presence, happily playing for hours.

TURKISH VAN

The Turkish Van is a rare, naturally occurring breed of cat from the Lake Van region of present-day Turkey. For Turkish Vans, the word van refers to their color pattern, where the color is restricted to the head and the tail, and the rest of the cat is white. The coat on a Van is considered semi-longhaired. While many cats have three distinct hair types in their coat - guard hairs, awn hairs and down hairs - the Turkish Van only has one. This makes their coat feel like cashmere or rabbit fur, and the coat dries quickly when wet. Lake Van is a region of temperature extremes and the cats have evolved a coat that grows thick in the winter with a large ruff and bottlebrush tail for the harsh winters and then sheds out short in the body for the warm summers. The full tail is kept year round. The Van is one of the larger cat breeds. The males can reach 20 lb (9 kg) and the females weigh about half of that. They have massive paws and rippling hard muscle structure which allows them to be very strong jumpers. Vans can easily hit the top of a refrigerator from a cold start on the floor. Perhaps the most interesting trait of the breed is its fascination with water; most cat breeds dislike being immersed in water. The unusual trait may be due to the breed's proximity to Lake Van in their native country; it may have acquired this trait due to the very hot summers and have extremely waterproof coats that make bathing them a challenge. As such, Vans have been nicknamed the "Swimming Cats" for this most unusual trait. Most Vans in the United States are indoor cats and do not have access to large bodies of water, but their love and curiosity of water stays with them. Instead of swimming they stir their water bowls and invent fishing games in the toilet.

INDEX